MznLnx

Missing Links Exam Preps

Exam Prep for

Understanding Management

Daft & Marcic, 4th Edition

The MznLnx Exam Prep is your link from the texbook and lecture to your exams.
The MznLnx Exam Preps are unauthorized and comprehensive reviews of your textbooks.

All material provided by MznLnx and Rico Publications (c) 2010
Textbook publishers and textbook authors do not particpate in or contribute to these reviews.

MznLnx

Rico
Publications

Exam Prep for Understanding Management
4th Edition
Daft & Marcic

Publisher: Raymond Houge
Assistant Editor: Michael Rouger
Text and Cover Designer: Lisa Buckner
Marketing Manager: Sara Swagger
Project Manager, Editorial Production: Jerry Emerson
Art Director: Vernon Lowerui

Product Manager: Dave Mason
Editorial Assitant: Rachel Guzmanji
Pedagogy: Debra Long
Cover Image: Jim Reed/Getty Images
Text and Cover Printer: City Printing, Inc.
Compositor: Media Mix, Inc.

(c) 2010 Rico Publications
ALL RIGHTS RESERVED. No part of this work covered by the copyright may be reproduced or used in any form or by an means--graphic, electronic, or mechanical, including photocopying, recording, taping, Web distribution, information storage, and retrieval systems, or in any other manner--without the written permission of the publisher.

Printed in the United States
ISBN:

For more information about our products, contact us at:
Dave.Mason@RicoPublications.com

For permission to use material from this text or product, submit a request online to:
Dave.Mason@RicoPublications.com

Contents

CHAPTER 1
Managing the New Workplace — 1

CHAPTER 2
The Environment and Corporate Culture — 15

CHAPTER 3
Managing in a Global Environment — 22

CHAPTER 4
Managerial Ethics and Corporate Social Responsibility — 30

CHAPTER 5
Organizational Planning and Goal Setting — 34

CHAPTER 6
Managerial Decision Making — 38

CHAPTER 7
Fundamentals of Organizing — 46

CHAPTER 8
Change and Development — 54

CHAPTER 9
Human Resource Management — 59

CHAPTER 10
Managing Diverse Employees — 73

CHAPTER 11
Foundations of Behavior in Organizations — 81

CHAPTER 12
Leadership in Organizations — 88

CHAPTER 13
Motivation in Organizations — 92

CHAPTER 14
Communicating in Organizations — 100

CHAPTER 15
Teamwork in Organizations — 102

CHAPTER 16
The Importance of Control — 107

ANSWER KEY — 118

TO THE STUDENT

COMPREHENSIVE

The *MznLnx* Exam Prep series is designed to help you pass your exams. Editors at MznLnx review your textbooks and then prepare these practice exams to help you master the textbook material. Unlike study guides, workbooks, and practice tests provided by the texbook publisher and textbook authors, *MznLnx* gives you **all** of the material in each chapter in exam form, not just samples, so you can be sure to nail your exam.

MECHANICAL

The MznLnx Exam Prep series creates exams that will help you learn the subject matter as well as test you on your understanding. Each question is designed to help you master the concept. Just working through the exams, you gain an understanding of the subject--its a simple mechanical process that produces success.

INTEGRATED STUDY GUIDE AND REVIEW

MznLnx is not just a set of exams designed to test you, its also a comprehensive review of the subject content. Each exam question is also a review of the concept, making sure that you will get the answer correct without having to go to other sources of material. You learn as you go! Its the easiest way to pass an exam.

HUMOR

Studying can be tedious and dry. MznLnx's instructional design includes moderate humor within the exam questions on occassion, to break the tedium and revitalize the brain

Chapter 1. Managing the New Workplace

1. A _____ is a list of the general tasks and responsibilities of a position. Typically, it also includes to whom the position reports, specifications such as the qualifications needed by the person in the job, salary range for the position, etc. A _____ is usually developed by conducting a job analysis, which includes examining the tasks and sequences of tasks necessary to perform the job.
    a. Job description
    b. Recruitment advertising
    c. Recruitment
    d. Recruitment Process Insourcing

2. A _____ is the belief that there is a technique, method, process, activity, incentive or reward that is more effective at delivering a particular outcome than any other technique, method, process, etc. The idea is that with proper processes, checks, and testing, a desired outcome can be delivered with fewer problems and unforeseen complications. _____s can also be defined as the most efficient (least amount of effort) and effective (best results) way of accomplishing a task, based on repeatable procedures that have proven themselves over time for large numbers of people.
    a. Fix it twice
    b. Hierarchical organization
    c. Design management
    d. Best practice

3. In economics, business, retail, and accounting, a _____ is the value of money that has been used up to produce something, and hence is not available for use anymore. In economics, a _____ is an alternative that is given up as a result of a decision. In business, the _____ may be one of acquisition, in which case the amount of money expended to acquire it is counted as _____.
    a. Fixed costs
    b. Cost overrun
    c. Cost allocation
    d. Cost

4. _____, in the context of parallel computer algorithms, refers to a measure of how effectively parallel computing can be used to solve a particular problem. A parallel algorithm is considered cost efficient if its asymptotic running time multiplied by the number of processing units involved in the computation is comparable to the running time of the best sequential algorithm.

For example, an algorithm that can be solved in O time using the best known sequential algorithm and $O\left(\dfrac{n}{p}\right)$ in a parallel computer with O(p) processors will be considered cost efficient.

a. WebFountain
b. Cost efficiency
c. 28-hour day
d. 1990 Clean Air Act

5. _____ is the concept of how effective an organization is in achieving the outcomes the organization intends to produce. The idea of _____ is especially important for non-profit organizations as most people who donate money to non-profit organizations and charities are interested in knowing whether the organization is effective in accomplishing its goals.

An organization's effectiveness is also dependent on its communicative competence and ethics.

a. Organizational structure
b. Informal organization
c. Organizational effectiveness
d. Organizational development

6. _____ in its literal sense is the process of transformation of local or regional phenomena into global ones. It can be described as a process by which the people of the world are unified into a single society and function together.

This process is a combination of economic, technological, sociocultural and political forces.

a. Histogram
b. Cost Management
c. Collaborative Planning, Forecasting and Replenishment
d. Globalization

7. A _____ is a business that is privately owned and operated, with a small number of employees and relatively low volume of sales. The legal definition of 'small' often varies by country and industry, but is generally under 100 employees in the United States and under 50 employees in the European Union. In comparison, the definition of mid-sized business by the number of employees is generally under 500 in the U.S. and 250 for the European Union.

a. Pre-determined overhead rate
b. Critical Success Factor
c. Golden Boot Compensation
d. Small business

8. _____, commonly known as e-commerce, consists of the buying and selling of products or services over electronic systems such as the Internet and other computer networks. The amount of trade conducted electronically has grown extraordinarily with widespread Internet usage. The use of commerce is conducted in this way, spurring and drawing on innovations in electronic funds transfer, supply chain management, Internet marketing, online transaction processing, electronic data interchange (EDI), inventory management systems, and automated data collection systems.

   a. A Stake in the Outcome
   b. A4e
   c. Online shopping
   d. Electronic Commerce

9. _____ refers to increasing the spiritual, political, social or economic strength of individuals and communities. It often involves the empowered developing confidence in their own capacities.

   The term Human _____ covers a vast landscape of meanings, interpretations, definitions and disciplines ranging from psychology and philosophy to the highly commercialized Self-Help industry and Motivational sciences.

   a. Empowerment
   b. A4e
   c. A Stake in the Outcome
   d. AAAI

10. In professional sports, a _____ is a team player whose contract with a team has expired, and the player is able to sign a contract with another team if that player is chosen. The term came into wide use in North America after sports leagues stopped using a 'reserve clause' after much acrimonious collective bargaining, which provided a repetitive option for the club to renew the contract for one more year, but did not allow the player to terminate the relationship with the team. The result of the reserve clause was abusive from the player standpoint so that a player was essentially property of the team.

    a. 33 Strategies of War
    b. 28-hour day
    c. 1990 Clean Air Act
    d. Free agent

11. _____, e-commuting, e-work, telework, working from home (WFH), or working at home (WAH) is a work arrangement in which employees enjoy flexibility in working location and hours. In other words, the daily commute to a central place of work is replaced by telecommunication links. Many work from home, while others, occasionally also referred to as nomad workers or web commuters utilize mobile telecommunications technology to work from coffee shops or myriad other locations.

a. 28-hour day
b. 1990 Clean Air Act
c. Telecommuting
d. 33 Strategies of War

12. _____, commonly referred to as 'eBusiness' or 'e-Business', may be defined as the utilization of information and communication technologies (ICT) in support of all the activities of business. Commerce constitutes the exchange of products and services between businesses, groups and individuals and hence can be seen as one of the essential activities of any business. Hence, electronic commerce or eCommerce focuses on the use of ICT to enable the external activities and relationships of the business with individuals, groups and other businesses .

a. AAAI
b. Electronic business
c. A Stake in the Outcome
d. A4e

13. An _____ is a private network that uses Internet protocols, network connectivity, and possibly the public telecommunication system to securely share part of an organization's information or operations with suppliers, vendors, partners, customers or other businesses. An _____ can be viewed as part of a company's intranet that is extended to users outside the company (e.g.: normally over the Internet.) It has also been described as a 'state of mind' in which the Internet is perceived as a way to do business with a preapproved set of other companies business-to-business (B2B), in isolation from all other Internet users.

a. A4e
b. A Stake in the Outcome
c. AAAI
d. Extranet

14. An _____ is a private computer network that uses Internet technologies to securely share any part of an organization's information or operational systems with its employees. Sometimes the term refers only to the organization's internal website, but often it is a more extensive part of the organization's computer infrastructure and private websites are an important component and focal point of internal communication and collaboration.

An _____ is built from the same concepts and technologies used for the Internet, such as client-server computing and the Internet Protocol Suite (TCP/IP.)

a. A4e
b. AAAI
c. A Stake in the Outcome
d. Intranet

15. _____, commonly abbreviated to Gen X, is a term used to refer to a generational cohort of children born after the baby boom ended and usually prior to the 1980s

The term _____ has been used in demography, the social sciences, and marketing, though it is most often used in popular culture.

In the U.S. _____ was originally referred to as the 'baby bust' generation because of the drop in the birth rate following the baby boom.

   a. Adam Smith
   b. Affiliation
   c. Abraham Harold Maslow
   d. Generation X

16. _____ is a term used to describe the demographic cohort following Generation X. Its members are often referred to as 'Millennials' or 'Echo Boomers') . There are no precise dates for when Gen Y begins and ends. Most commentators use dates from the early 1980s to early 1990s.
   a. David Wittig
   b. Benjamin R. Barber
   c. Giovanni Agnelli
   d. Generation Y

17. _____ has been described as the 'process of social influence in which one person can enlist the aid and support of others in the accomplishment of a common task' . A definition more inclusive of followers comes from Alan Keith of Genentech who said '_____ is ultimately about creating a way for people to contribute to making something extraordinary happen.'

_____ is one of the most salient aspects of the organizational context. However, defining _____ has been challenging.

   a. 1990 Clean Air Act
   b. Leadership
   c. 28-hour day
   d. Situational leadership

18. The 'business case for _____', theorizes that in a global marketplace, a company that employs a diverse workforce (both men and women, people of many generations, people from ethnically and racially diverse backgrounds etc.) is better able to understand the demographics of the marketplace it serves and is thus better equipped to thrive in that marketplace than a company that has a more limited range of employee demographics.

An additional corollary suggests that a company that supports the _____ of its workforce can also improve employee satisfaction, productivity and retention.

a. Trademark
b. Virtual team
c. Diversity
d. Kanban

19. The _____ is the labour pool in employment. It is generally used to describe those working for a single company or industry, but can also apply to a geographic region like a city, country, state, etc. The term generally excludes the employers or management, and implies those involved in manual labour.
a. Pink-collar worker
b. Division of labour
c. Work-life balance
d. Workforce

20. _____ is the process by which an organization deals with any major unpredictable event that threatens to harm the organization, its stakeholders, or the general public. Three elements are common to most definitions of crisis: (a) a threat to the organization, (b) the element of surprise, and (c) a short decision time.

Whereas risk management involves assessing potential threats and finding the best ways to avoid those threats, _____ involves dealing with the disasters after they have occurred.

a. Business value
b. Capability management
c. C-A-K-E
d. Crisis management

21. A _____ is the term given to a company that facilitates the learning of its members and continuously transforms itself. _____s develop as a result of the pressures facing modern organizations and enables them to remain competitive in the business environment. A _____ has five main features; systems thinking, personal mastery, mental models, shared vision and team learning.
a. Hoshin Kanri
b. 1990 Clean Air Act
c. Quality function deployment
d. Learning organization

Chapter 1. Managing the New Workplace

22. There are two types of _____ relationships: formal and informal. Informal relationships develop on their own between partners. Formal _____, on the other hand, refers to assigned relationships, often associated with organizational _____ programs designed to promote employee development or to assist at-risk children and youth.
    a. Human resource management system
    b. Real Property Administrator
    c. Fix it twice
    d. Mentoring

23. _____ is a theory of management that analyzes and synthesizes workflows, with the objective of improving labour productivity. The core ideas of the theory were developed by Frederick Winslow Taylor in the 1880s and 1890s, and were first published in his monographs, Shop Management and The Principles of _____ Taylor believed that decisions based upon tradition and rules of thumb should be replaced by precise procedures developed after careful study of an individual at work.
    a. Value engineering
    b. Capacity planning
    c. Scientific management
    d. Master production schedule

24. _____ describes commerce transactions between businesses, such as between a manufacturer and a wholesaler, or between a wholesaler and a retailer. Contrasting terms are business-to-consumer (B2C) and business-to-government (B2G.)

    The volume of B2B transactions is much higher than the volume of B2C transactions.

    a. Category management
    b. Business-to-business
    c. Market environment
    d. Product bundling

25. A _____ -- also known as a geographically dispersed team -- is a group of individuals who work across time, space, and organizational boundaries with links strengthened by webs of communication technology. They have complementary skills and are committed to a common purpose, have interdependent performance goals, and share an approach to work for which they hold themselves mutually accountable. Geographically dispersed teams allow organizations to hire and retain the best people regardless of location.
    a. Trademark
    b. Risk management
    c. Kanban
    d. Virtual team

26. _____ is a company-wide computer software system used to manage and coordinate all the resources, information, and functions of a business from shared data stores.

An _____ system has a service-oriented architecture with modular hardware and software units and 'services' that communicate on a local area network. The modular design allows a business to add or reconfigure modules (perhaps from different vendors) while preserving data integrity in one shared database that may be centralized or distributed.

   a. AAAI
   b. Enterprise resource planning
   c. A Stake in the Outcome
   d. A4e

27. _____ comprises a range of practices used in an organisation to identify, create, represent, distribute and enable adoption of insights and experiences. Such insights and experiences comprise knowledge, either embodied in individuals or embedded in organisational processes or practice.

An established discipline since 1991, _____ includes courses taught in the fields of business administration, information systems, management, and library and information sciences.

   a. 28-hour day
   b. Knowledge management
   c. 1990 Clean Air Act
   d. 33 Strategies of War

28. _____ is an economic and social system in which trade and industry are privately controlled for profit. The means of production, which is otherwise known as capital and includes land are owned, operated, and traded for the purpose of generating profits, without force or fraud, by private individuals either singly or jointly. Investments, distribution, income, production, pricing and supply of goods, commodities and services are determined by voluntary private decision in _____, which is also known as a market economy.

   a. Affiliation
   b. Abraham Harold Maslow
   c. Adam Smith
   d. Capitalism

29. _____ is a management technique pioneered by Michael Phillips in San Francisco in the late '60's and early '70s. The concept's most visible success was by Jack Stack and his team at SRC Holdings and popularized in 1995 by John Case. The technique is to give employees all relevant financial information about the company so they can make better decisions as workers.

a. A4e
b. A Stake in the Outcome
c. AAAI
d. Open-book management

30. _____, is the discipline of using scientific research-based principles, strategies, and other analytical methods, such as mathematical modeling to improve any organization's ability to enact rational, meaningful business management decisions.
a. Cross ownership
b. Trustee
c. Management science
d. Workflow

31. The _____ was an evolution of developed countries from an industrial/manufacturing-based wealth producing economy into a service sector asset based economy, brought about by globalization and currency manipulation by governments and their central banks. Some analysts claimed that this change in the economic structure of the United States had created a state of permanent steady growth, low unemployment, and immunity to boom and bust macroeconomic cycles. They believed that the change rendered obsolete many business practices.
a. 1990 Clean Air Act
b. New economy
c. 33 Strategies of War
d. 28-hour day

32. _____ is a business management strategy aimed at embedding awareness of quality in all organizational processes. _____ has been widely used in manufacturing, education, hospitals, call centers, government, and service industries, as well as NASA space and science programs.

As defined by the International Organization for Standardization (ISO):

> '_____ is a management approach for an organization, centered on quality, based on the participation of all its members and aiming at long-term success through customer satisfaction, and benefits to all members of the organization and to society.' ISO 8402:1994

One major aim is to reduce variation from every process so that greater consistency of effort is obtained. (Royse, D., Thyer, B., Padgett D., ' Logan T., 2006)

Chapter 1. Managing the New Workplace

a. 1990 Clean Air Act
b. Total quality management
c. 28-hour day
d. Quality management

33. _____ can be considered to have three main components: quality control, quality assurance and quality improvement. _____ is focused not only on product quality, but also the means to achieve it. _____ therefore uses quality assurance and control of processes as well as products to achieve more consistent quality.
   a. 28-hour day
   b. Quality management
   c. Total quality management
   d. 1990 Clean Air Act

34. _____ or specialization is the specialization of cooperative labour in specific, circumscribed tasks and roles, intended to increase the productivity of labour. Historically the growth of a more and more complex _____ is closely associated with the growth of total output and trade, the rise of capitalism, and of the complexity of industrialization processes. Later, the _____ reached the level of a scientifically-based management practice with the time and motion studies associated with Taylorism.
   a. Labor force
   b. Departmentalization
   c. PATCOB
   d. Division of labour

35. The _____ is a standardized, on-scene, all-hazard incident management concept. It is a management protocol originally designed for emergency management agencies in the United States which was later federalized there. It has since been adopted by agencies in other countries.
   a. A4e
   b. Incident Command Structure
   c. A Stake in the Outcome
   d. AAAI

36. _____ is an organization's process of defining its strategy and making decisions on allocating its resources to pursue this strategy, including its capital and people. Various business analysis techniques can be used in _____, including SWOT analysis (Strengths, Weaknesses, Opportunities, and Threats) and PEST analysis (Political, Economic, Social, and Technological analysis) or STEER analysis involving Socio-cultural, Technological, Economic, Ecological, and Regulatory factors and EPISTEL (Environment, Political, Informatic, Social, Technological, Economic and Legal)

_____ is the formal consideration of an organization's future course. All _____ deals with at least one of three key questions:

1. 'What do we do?'
2. 'For whom do we do it?'
3. 'How do we excel?'

In business _____, the third question is better phrased 'How can we beat or avoid competition?'. (Bradford and Duncan, page 1.)

   a. 1990 Clean Air Act
   b. 33 Strategies of War
   c. 28-hour day
   d. Strategic planning

37. _____ Movement refers to those researchers of organizational development who study the behavior of people in groups, in particular workplace groups. It originated in the 1920s' Hawthorne studies, which examined the effects of social relations, motivation and employee satisfaction on factory productivity. The movement viewed workers in terms of their psychology and fit with companies, rather than as interchangeable parts.
   a. Participatory management
   b. Work design
   c. Human Relations
   d. Hersey-Blanchard situational theory

38. _____ refers to those researchers of organizational development who study the behavior of people in groups, in particular workplace groups. It originated in the 1920s' Hawthorne studies, which examined the effects of social relations, motivation and employee satisfaction on factory productivity. The movement viewed workers in terms of their psychology and fit with companies, rather than as interchangeable parts.
   a. Job analysis
   b. Path-goal theory
   c. Job satisfaction
   d. Human Relations Movement

39. The _____ is the interlocking social structure that governs how people work together in practice. It is the aggregate of behaviors, interactions, norms, personal and professional connections through which work gets done and relationships are built among people who share a common organizational affiliation or cluster of affiliations. It consists of a dynamic set of personal relationships, social networks, communities of common interest, and emotional sources of motivation. The _____ evolves organically and spontaneously in response to changes in the work environment, the flux of people through its porous boundaries, and the complex social dynamics of its members.

a. Informal organization
b. Open shop
c. Union shop
d. Organizational effectiveness

40. The _____ is a form of reactivity whereby subjects improve an aspect of their behavior being experimentally measured simply in response to the fact that they are being studied, not in response to any particular experimental manipulation.

The term was coined in 1955 by Henry A. Landsberger when analyzing older experiments from 1924-1932 at the Hawthorne Works (outside Chicago.) Hawthorne Works had commissioned a study to see if its workers would become more productive in higher or lower levels of light.

a. 1990 Clean Air Act
b. 28-hour day
c. 33 Strategies of War
d. Hawthorne effect

41. _____ and Theory Y are theories of human motivation created and developed by Douglas McGregor at the MIT Sloan School of Management in the 1960s that have been used in human resource management, organizational behavior, organizational communication and organizational development. They describe two very different attitudes toward workforce motivation. McGregor felt that companies followed either one or the other approach.

In _____, which many managers practice, management assumes employees are inherently lazy and will avoid work if they can. They inherently dislike work. Because of this, workers need to be closely supervised and comprehensive systems of controls developed.

a. Job enrichment
b. Management team
c. Cash cow
d. Theory X

42. Theory X and _____ are theories of human motivation created and developed by Douglas McGregor at the MIT Sloan School of Management in the 1960s that have been used in human resource management, organizational behavior, organizational communication and organizational development. They describe two very different attitudes toward workforce motivation. McGregor felt that companies followed either one or the other approach.

In _____, management assumes employees may be ambitious and self-motivated and exercise self-control. It is believed that employees enjoy their mental and physical work duties.

a. Contingency theory
b. Business Workflow Analysis
c. Design leadership
d. Theory Y

43. _____ is an increasingly broadening term with which an organization, or other human system describes the combination of traditionally administrative personnel functions with acquisition and application of skills, knowledge and experience, Employee Relations and resource planning at various levels. The field draws upon concepts developed in Industrial/Organizational Psychology and System Theory. _____ has at least two related interpretations depending on context. The original usage derives from political economy and economics, where it was traditionally called labor, one of four factors of production although this perspective is changing as a function of new and ongoing research into more strategic approaches at national levels. This first usage is used more in terms of '_____ development', and can go beyond just organizations to the level of nations. The more traditional usage within corporations and businesses refers to the individuals within a firm or agency, and to the portion of the organization that deals with hiring, firing, training, and other personnel issues, typically referred to as `_____ management'.

   a. Human resource management
   b. Progressive discipline
   c. Bradford Factor
   d. Human resources

44. _____ is the process of comparing the cost, cycle time, productivity, or quality of a specific process or method to another that is widely considered to be an industry standard or best practice. Essentially, _____ provides a snapshot of the performance of your business and helps you understand where you are in relation to a particular standard. The result is often a business case for making changes in order to make improvements.

   a. Competitive heterogeneity
   b. Cost leadership
   c. Complementors
   d. Benchmarking

45. In business and accounting, _____s are everything of value that is owned by a person or company. Any property or object of value that one possesses, usually considered as applicable to the payment of one's debts is considered an _____. Simplistically stated, _____s are things of value that can be readily converted into cash.

   a. AAAI
   b. A4e
   c. A Stake in the Outcome
   d. Asset

46. _____ is a contract between two parties, one being the employer and the other being the employee. An employee may be defined as: 'A person in the service of another under any contract of hire, express or implied, oral or written, where the employer has the power or right to control and direct the employee in the material details of how the work is to be performed.' Black's Law Dictionary page 471 (5th ed. 1979.)
   a. Employment counsellor
   b. Employment
   c. Exit interview
   d. Employment rate

47. A _____ is a research instrument consisting of a series of questions and other prompts for the purpose of gathering information from respondents. Although they are often designed for statistical analysis of the responses, this is not always the case. The _____ was invented by Sir Francis Galton.
   a. Questionnaire construction
   b. Mystery shoppers
   c. Questionnaire
   d. Structured interview

Chapter 2. The Environment and Corporate Culture

1. A _____ or transnational corporation is a corporation or enterprise that manages production or delivers services in more than one country. It can also be referred to as an international corporation.

   The first modern _____ is generally thought to be the Dutch East India Company, established in 1602.

   a. Command center
   b. Multinational Corporation
   c. Financial Accounting Standards Board
   d. Small and medium enterprises

2. _____ is a form of communication that typically attempts to persuade potential customers to purchase or to consume more of a particular brand of product or service. 'While now central to the contemporary global economy and the reproduction of global production networks, it is only quite recently that _____ has been more than a marginal influence on patterns of sales and production. The formation of modern _____ was intimately bound up with the emergence of new forms of monopoly capitalism around the end of the 19th and beginning of the 20th century as one element in corporate strategies to create, organize and where possible control markets, especially for mass produced consumer goods.
   a. A4e
   b. A Stake in the Outcome
   c. Advertising
   d. AAAI

3. _____ in its literal sense is the process of transformation of local or regional phenomena into global ones. It can be described as a process by which the people of the world are unified into a single society and function together.

   This process is a combination of economic, technological, sociocultural and political forces.

   a. Collaborative Planning, Forecasting and Replenishment
   b. Histogram
   c. Cost Management
   d. Globalization

4. _____ is the removal or simplification of government rules and regulations that constrain the operation of market forces. _____ does not mean elimination of laws against fraud, but eliminating or reducing government control of how business is done, thereby moving toward a more free market.

   The stated rationale for '_____' is often that fewer and simpler regulations will lead to a raised level of competitiveness, therefore higher productivity, more efficiency and lower prices overall.

a. Rehn-Meidner Model
b. Value added
c. Natural rate of unemployment
d. Deregulation

5. _____ is a contract between two parties, one being the employer and the other being the employee. An employee may be defined as: 'A person in the service of another under any contract of hire, express or implied, oral or written, where the employer has the power or right to control and direct the employee in the material details of how the work is to be performed.' Black's Law Dictionary page 471 (5th ed. 1979.)
   a. Employment counsellor
   b. Employment rate
   c. Exit interview
   d. Employment

6. In economics, _____ is a measure of the relative satisfaction from consumption of various goods and services. Given this measure, one may speak meaningfully of increasing or decreasing _____, and thereby explain economic behavior in terms of attempts to increase one's _____. For illustrative purposes, changes in _____ are sometimes expressed in units called utils.
   a. Indirect utility function
   b. A Stake in the Outcome
   c. Utility
   d. Ordinal utility

7. _____ is the statistical study of all populations. It can be a very general science that can be applied to any kind of dynamic population, that is, one that changes over time or space It encompasses the study of the size, structure and distribution of populations, and spatial and/or temporal changes in them in response to birth, migration, aging and death.
   a. 33 Strategies of War
   b. 28-hour day
   c. 1990 Clean Air Act
   d. Demography

8. _____, commonly referred to as 'eBusiness' or 'e-Business', may be defined as the utilization of information and communication technologies (ICT) in support of all the activities of business. Commerce constitutes the exchange of products and services between businesses, groups and individuals and hence can be seen as one of the essential activities of any business. Hence, electronic commerce or eCommerce focuses on the use of ICT to enable the external activities and relationships of the business with individuals, groups and other businesses .

a. A Stake in the Outcome
b. AAAI
c. A4e
d. Electronic business

9. _____ is a term used to describe the demographic cohort following Generation X. Its members are often referred to as 'Millennials' or 'Echo Boomers') . There are no precise dates for when Gen Y begins and ends. Most commentators use dates from the early 1980s to early 1990s.
   a. Giovanni Agnelli
   b. David Wittig
   c. Benjamin R. Barber
   d. Generation Y

10. A _____ is a relatively new executive level position at a corporation, company, organization typically reporting directly to the CEO or board of directors. The _____ is responsible for a brand's image, experience, and promise, and propagating it throughout all aspects of the company. The brand officer oversees marketing, advertising, design, public relations and customer service departments.
   a. Director of communications
   b. Chief executive officer
   c. Purchasing manager
   d. Chief brand officer

11. _____ is technology based on biology, especially when used in agriculture, food science, and medicine. United Nations Convention on Biological Diversity defines _____ as:

_____ is often used to refer to genetic engineering technology of the 21st century, however the term encompasses a wider range and history of procedures for modifying biological organisms according to the needs of humanity, going back to the initial modifications of native plants into improved food crops through artificial selection and hybridization. Bioengineering is the science upon which all biotechnological applications are based.

   a. 1990 Clean Air Act
   b. Biotechnology
   c. 28-hour day
   d. 33 Strategies of War

12. The phrase _____ refers to the aspect of corporate strategy, corporate finance and management dealing with the buying, selling and combining of different companies that can aid, finance, or help a growing company in a given industry grow rapidly without having to create another business entity.

An acquisition, also known as a takeover or a buyout, is the buying of one company (the 'target') by another. An acquisition may be friendly or hostile.

a. 1990 Clean Air Act
b. 33 Strategies of War
c. 28-hour day
d. Mergers and acquisitions

13. _____ is a cross-disciplinary area concerned with protecting the safety, health and welfare of people engaged in work or employment. The goal of all _____ programs is to foster a work free safe environment. As a secondary effect, it may also protect co-workers, family members, employers, customers, suppliers, nearby communities, and other members of the public who are impacted by the workplace environment.
a. AAAI
b. A Stake in the Outcome
c. A4e
d. Occupational Safety and Health

14. The United States _____ is an agency of the United States Department of Labor. It was created by Congress under the Occupational Safety and Health Act, signed by President Richard M. Nixon, on December 29, 1970. Its mission is to prevent work-related injuries, illnesses, and deaths by issuing and enforcing rules (called standards) for workplace safety and health.
a. Unemployment insurance
b. Opinion leadership
c. Operant conditioning
d. Occupational Safety and Health Administration

15. The _____ is an international organization designed by its founders to supervise and liberalize international trade. The organization officially commenced on 1 January 1995, under the Marrakesh Agreement, succeeding the 1947 General Agreement on Tariffs and Trade (GATT.)

The _____ deals with regulation of trade between participating countries; it provides a framework for negotiating and formalising trade agreements, and a dispute resolution process aimed at enforcing participants' adherence to _____ agreements which are signed by representatives of member governments and ratified by their parliaments.

a. 1990 Clean Air Act
b. National Institute for Occupational Safety and Health
c. Network planning and design
d. World Trade Organization

16. The phrase mergers and _____s refers to the aspect of corporate strategy, corporate finance and management dealing with the buying, selling and combining of different companies that can aid, finance, or help a growing company in a given industry grow rapidly without having to create another business entity.

An _____, also known as a takeover or a buyout, is the buying of one company (the 'target') by another. An _____ may be friendly or hostile.

a. AAAI
b. A4e
c. A Stake in the Outcome
d. Acquisition

17. _____ is the observation that people often do and believe things because many other people do and believe the same things. The effect is often called herd instinct. People tend to follow the crowd without examining the merits of a particular thing.
a. Choice-supportive bias
b. Bandwagon effect
c. Confirmation bias
d. Distinction bias

18. The term '_____' refers to the concept of collecting information and attempting to spot a pattern in the information. In some fields of study, the term '_____' has more formally-defined meanings.

In project management _____ is a mathematical technique that uses historical results to predict future outcome.

a. Regression analysis
b. Stepwise regression
c. Least squares
d. Trend analysis

Chapter 2. The Environment and Corporate Culture

19. _____, commonly known as e-commerce, consists of the buying and selling of products or services over electronic systems such as the Internet and other computer networks. The amount of trade conducted electronically has grown extraordinarily with widespread Internet usage. The use of commerce is conducted in this way, spurring and drawing on innovations in electronic funds transfer, supply chain management, Internet marketing, online transaction processing, electronic data interchange (EDI), inventory management systems, and automated data collection systems.
    a. A Stake in the Outcome
    b. A4e
    c. Electronic Commerce
    d. Online shopping

20. Organizational culture is not the same as _____. It is wider and deeper concepts, something that an organization 'is' rather than what it 'has' (according to Buchanan and Huczynski.)

    _____ is the total sum of the values, customs, traditions and meanings that make a company unique.

    a. Job analysis
    b. Path-goal theory
    c. Corporate culture
    d. Work design

21. A _____ is the belief that there is a technique, method, process, activity, incentive or reward that is more effective at delivering a particular outcome than any other technique, method, process, etc. The idea is that with proper processes, checks, and testing, a desired outcome can be delivered with fewer problems and unforeseen complications. _____s can also be defined as the most efficient (least amount of effort) and effective (best results) way of accomplishing a task, based on repeatable procedures that have proven themselves over time for large numbers of people.
    a. Fix it twice
    b. Design management
    c. Hierarchical organization
    d. Best practice

22. _____, e-commuting, e-work, telework, working from home (WFH), or working at home (WAH) is a work arrangement in which employees enjoy flexibility in working location and hours. In other words, the daily commute to a central place of work is replaced by telecommunication links. Many work from home, while others, occasionally also referred to as nomad workers or web commuters utilize mobile telecommunications technology to work from coffee shops or myriad other locations.

Chapter 2. The Environment and Corporate Culture 21

   a. 1990 Clean Air Act
   b. Telecommuting
   c. 33 Strategies of War
   d. 28-hour day

23. _____ has been described as the 'process of social influence in which one person can enlist the aid and support of others in the accomplishment of a common task' . A definition more inclusive of followers comes from Alan Keith of Genentech who said '_____ is ultimately about creating a way for people to contribute to making something extraordinary happen.'

_____ is one of the most salient aspects of the organizational context. However, defining _____ has been challenging.

   a. Situational leadership
   b. 1990 Clean Air Act
   c. Leadership
   d. 28-hour day

24. In economics, business, retail, and accounting, a _____ is the value of money that has been used up to produce something, and hence is not available for use anymore. In economics, a _____ is an alternative that is given up as a result of a decision. In business, the _____ may be one of acquisition, in which case the amount of money expended to acquire it is counted as _____.
   a. Fixed costs
   b. Cost overrun
   c. Cost allocation
   d. Cost

Chapter 3. Managing in a Global Environment

1. _____ in its literal sense is the process of transformation of local or regional phenomena into global ones. It can be described as a process by which the people of the world are unified into a single society and function together.

This process is a combination of economic, technological, sociocultural and political forces.

   a. Cost Management
   b. Collaborative Planning, Forecasting and Replenishment
   c. Histogram
   d. Globalization

2. _____ is a contract between two parties, one being the employer and the other being the employee. An employee may be defined as: 'A person in the service of another under any contract of hire, express or implied, oral or written, where the employer has the power or right to control and direct the employee in the material details of how the work is to be performed.' Black's Law Dictionary page 471 (5th ed. 1979.)
   a. Exit interview
   b. Employment rate
   c. Employment
   d. Employment counsellor

3. _____ is a field of study that looks at how people from differing cultural backgrounds endeavour to communicate.

In years during and preceding the Cold War, the United States economy was largely self-contained because the world was polarized into two separate and competing powers: the east and west. However, changes and advancements in economic relationships, political systems, and technological options began to break down old cultural barriers.

   a. Cross-cultural communication
   b. 33 Strategies of War
   c. 28-hour day
   d. 1990 Clean Air Act

4. _____ means how much each individual receives, in monetary terms, of the yearly income generated in the country. This is what each citizen is to receive if the yearly national income is divided equally among everyone. _____ is usually reported in units of currency per year.
   a. 28-hour day
   b. 1990 Clean Air Act
   c. 33 Strategies of War
   d. Per capita income

Chapter 3. Managing in a Global Environment

5. In finance, the _____s between two currencies specifies how much one currency is worth in terms of the other. It is the value of a foreign nation's currency in terms of the home nation's currency. For example an _____ of 102 Japanese yen to the United States dollar means that JPY 102 is worth the same as USD 1.
   a. A Stake in the Outcome
   b. AAAI
   c. A4e
   d. Exchange rate

6. _____ is a type of trade policy that allows traders to act and transact without interference from government. Thus, the policy permits trading partners mutual gains from trade, with goods and services produced according to the theory of comparative advantage.

   Under a _____ policy, prices are a reflection of true supply and demand, and are the sole determinant of resource allocation.

   a. 28-hour day
   b. 1990 Clean Air Act
   c. 33 Strategies of War
   d. Free Trade

7. _____ is a designated group of countries that have agreed to eliminate tariffs, quotas and preferences on most (if not all) goods and services traded between them. It can be considered the second stage of economic integration. Countries choose this kind of economic integration form if their economical structures are complementary.
   a. 1990 Clean Air Act
   b. 33 Strategies of War
   c. 28-hour day
   d. Free trade area

8. The _____ was the outcome of the failure of negotiating governments to create the International Trade Organization (ITO.) GATT was formed in 1947 and lasted until 1994, when it was replaced by the World Trade Organization. The Bretton Woods Conference had introduced the idea for an organization to regulate trade as part of a larger plan for economic recovery after World War II.
   a. Multilateral treaty
   b. 1990 Clean Air Act
   c. 28-hour day
   d. General Agreement on Tariffs and Trade

Chapter 3. Managing in a Global Environment

9. The _____ is a trilateral trade bloc in North America created by the governments of the United States, Canada, and Mexico. The agreement creating the trade bloc came into force on January 1, 1994. It superseded the Canada-United States Free Trade Agreement between the U.S. and Canada.
   a. Trade union
   b. Career portfolios
   c. Business war game
   d. North American Free Trade Agreement

10. The _____ is an international organization designed by its founders to supervise and liberalize international trade. The organization officially commenced on 1 January 1995, under the Marrakesh Agreement, succeeding the 1947 General Agreement on Tariffs and Trade (GATT.)

    The _____ deals with regulation of trade between participating countries; it provides a framework for negotiating and formalising trade agreements, and a dispute resolution process aimed at enforcing participants' adherence to _____ agreements which are signed by representatives of member governments and ratified by their parliaments.

    a. 1990 Clean Air Act
    b. Network planning and design
    c. National Institute for Occupational Safety and Health
    d. World Trade Organization

11. In decision theory and estimation theory, the _____ of an estimator, $\hat{\theta}$, of an unknown parameter of the distribution, θ, is the expected value of the loss function

$$R(\theta, \hat{\theta}) = \mathbb{E}_\theta L(\theta, \hat{\theta}) = \int L(\theta, \hat{\theta})\, dP_\theta.$$

where dP_θ is a probability measure parametrized by θ.

- For a scalar parameter θ and a quadratic loss function,

$$L(\theta, \hat{\theta}) = (\theta - \hat{\theta})^2$$

the _____ function becomes the mean squared error of the estimate,

$$R(\theta, \hat{\theta}) = E_\theta (\theta - \hat{\theta})^2$$

- In density estimation, the unknown parameter is probability density itself. The loss function is typically chosen to be a norm in an appropriate function space. For example, for L^2 norm,

$$L(f, \hat{f}) = \|f - \hat{f}\|_2^2$$

the _____ function becomes the mean integrated squared error

$$R(f, \hat{f}) = E\|f - \hat{f}\|^2$$

a. Risk
b. Linear model
c. Financial modeling
d. Risk aversion

12. A _____ is a set of consistent ethic values (more specifically the personal and cultural values) and measures used for the purpose of ethical or ideological integrity. A well defined _____ is a moral code.

Fred Wenst>øp and Arild Myrmel have proposed a structure for corporate _____s that consists of three value categories. These are considered complementary and juxtaposed on the same level if illustrated graphically on for instance an organization's web page. The first value category is Core Values, which prescribe the attitude and character of an organization, and are often found in sections on Code of conduct on its web page. The philosophical antecedents of these values are Virtue ethics, which is often attributed to Aristotle. Protected Values are protected through rules, standards and certifications. They are often concerned with areas such as health, environment and safety. The third category, Created Values, is the values that stakeholders, including the shareholders expect in return for their contributions to the firm. These values are subject to trade-off by decision-makers or bargaining processes. This process is explained further in Stakeholder theory.

a. 1990 Clean Air Act
b. Value system
c. 33 Strategies of War
d. 28-hour day

13. _____ is a term used to describe any moral, political that stresses human interdependence and the importance of a collective, rather than the importance of separate individuals. Collectivists focus on community and society, and seek to give priority to group goals over individual goals. The philosophical underpinnings of _____ are for some related to holism or organicism - the view that the whole is greater than the sum of its parts/pieces.
    a. Collaborative methods
    b. 28-hour day
    c. 1990 Clean Air Act
    d. Collectivism

14. _____, commonly referred to as 'eBusiness' or 'e-Business', may be defined as the utilization of information and communication technologies (ICT) in support of all the activities of business. Commerce constitutes the exchange of products and services between businesses, groups and individuals and hence can be seen as one of the essential activities of any business. Hence, electronic commerce or eCommerce focuses on the use of ICT to enable the external activities and relationships of the business with individuals, groups and other businesses .
    a. A Stake in the Outcome
    b. A4e
    c. AAAI
    d. Electronic business

15. A _____ strategy is the planned method of delivering goods or services to a target market and distributing them there. When importing or exporting services, it refers to establishing and managing contracts in a foreign country.

Many companies successfully operate in a niche market without ever expanding into new markets.

    a. Foreign ownership
    b. Market entry
    c. Psychological pricing
    d. Horizontal integration

Chapter 3. Managing in a Global Environment

16. _____ is one of the managerial functions like planning, organizing, staffing and directing. It is an important function because it helps to check the errors and to take the corrective action so that deviation from standards are minimized and stated goals of the organization are achieved in desired manner. According to modern concepts, _____ is a foreseeing action whereas earlier concept of _____ was used only when errors were detected. _____ in management means setting standards, measuring actual performance and taking corrective action.
   a. Turnover
   b. Schedule of reinforcement
   c. Control
   d. Decision tree pruning

17. _____ is subcontracting a process, such as product design or manufacturing, to a third-party company. The decision to outsource is often made in the interest of lowering cost or making better use of time and energy costs, redirecting or conserving energy directed at the competencies of a particular business, or to make more efficient use of land, labor, capital, (information) technology and resources. _____ became part of the business lexicon during the 1980s.
   a. Unemployment insurance
   b. Opinion leadership
   c. Outsourcing
   d. Operant conditioning

18. _____ is exchange of capital, goods, and services across international borders or territories. In most countries, it represents a significant share of gross domestic product (GDP.) While _____ has been present throughout much of history, its economic, social, and political importance has been on the rise in recent centuries.
   a. A Stake in the Outcome
   b. AAAI
   c. International trade
   d. A4e

19. A _____ or maquila is a factory that imports materials and equipment on a duty-free and tariff-free basis for assembly or manufacturing and then re-exports the assembled product, usually back to the originating country. A maquila is also referred to as a 'twin plant', or 'in-bond' industry. Nearly half a million Mexicans are employed in _____s.
   a. Maquiladora
   b. 33 Strategies of War
   c. 1990 Clean Air Act
   d. 28-hour day

20. A _____ is the belief that there is a technique, method, process, activity, incentive or reward that is more effective at delivering a particular outcome than any other technique, method, process, etc. The idea is that with proper processes, checks, and testing, a desired outcome can be delivered with fewer problems and unforeseen complications. _____s can also be defined as the most efficient (least amount of effort) and effective (best results) way of accomplishing a task, based on repeatable procedures that have proven themselves over time for large numbers of people.

   a. Design management
   b. Hierarchical organization
   c. Fix it twice
   d. Best practice

21. _____ refers to the methods of practicing and using another person's business philosophy. The franchisor grants the independent operator the right to distribute its products, techniques, and trademarks for a percentage of gross monthly sales and a royalty fee. Various tangibles and intangibles such as national or international advertising, training, and other support services are commonly made available by the franchisor.

   a. ServiceMaster
   b. 1990 Clean Air Act
   c. 28-hour day
   d. Franchising

22. A _____ is an entity formed between two or more parties to undertake economic activity together. The parties agree to create a new entity by both contributing equity, and they then share in the revenues, expenses, and control of the enterprise. The venture can be for one specific project only, or a continuing business relationship such as the Fuji Xerox _____.

   a. Civil Rights Act of 1991
   b. Meritor Savings Bank v. Vinson
   c. Patent
   d. Joint venture

23. A _____ or transnational corporation is a corporation or enterprise that manages production or delivers services in more than one country. It can also be referred to as an international corporation.

The first modern _____ is generally thought to be the Dutch East India Company, established in 1602.

   a. Command center
   b. Small and medium enterprises
   c. Financial Accounting Standards Board
   d. Multinational Corporation

Chapter 3. Managing in a Global Environment

24. An _____ is a person who has possession of an enterprise and assumes significant accountability for the inherent risks and the outcome. It is an ambitious leader who combines land, labor, and capital to create and market new goods or services. The term is a loanword from French and was first defined by the Irish economist Richard Cantillon.
   a. AAAI
   b. A Stake in the Outcome
   c. A4e
   d. Entrepreneur

25. _____ has been described as the 'process of social influence in which one person can enlist the aid and support of others in the accomplishment of a common task' . A definition more inclusive of followers comes from Alan Keith of Genentech who said '_____ is ultimately about creating a way for people to contribute to making something extraordinary happen.'

   _____ is one of the most salient aspects of the organizational context. However, defining _____ has been challenging.

   a. 28-hour day
   b. 1990 Clean Air Act
   c. Leadership
   d. Situational leadership

26. _____ can be regarded as an outcome of mental processes (cognitive process) leading to the selection of a course of action among several alternatives. Every _____ process produces a final choice. The output can be an action or an opinion of choice.
   a. 28-hour day
   b. 1990 Clean Air Act
   c. 33 Strategies of War
   d. Decision making

Chapter 4. Managerial Ethics and Corporate Social Responsibility

1. _____ is a form of corporate self-regulation integrated into a business model. Ideally, _____ policy would function as a built-in, self-regulating mechanism whereby business would monitor and ensure their adherence to law, ethical standards, and international norms. Business would embrace responsibility for the impact of their activities on the environment, consumers, employees, communities, stakeholders and all other members of the public sphere.
    a. 1990 Clean Air Act
    b. 33 Strategies of War
    c. 28-hour day
    d. Corporate social responsibility

2. The general definition of an _____ is an evaluation of a person, organization, system, process, project or product. _____s are performed to ascertain the validity and reliability of information; also to provide an assessment of a system's internal control. The goal of an _____ is to express an opinion on the person / organization/system (etc) in question, under evaluation based on work done on a test basis.
    a. Internal control
    b. A Stake in the Outcome
    c. Audit
    d. Audit committee

3. An _____ is a situation that will often involve an apparent conflict between moral imperatives, in which to obey one would result in transgressing another. This is also called an ethical paradox since in moral philosophy, paradox plays a central role in ethics debates. For instance, an ethical admonition to 'love thy neighbour as thy self' is not always just in contrast with, but sometimes in contradiction to an armed neighbour actively trying to kill you: if he or she succeeds, you will not be able to love him or her.
    a. A4e
    b. AAAI
    c. A Stake in the Outcome
    d. Ethical dilemma

4. _____ can be regarded as an outcome of mental processes (cognitive process) leading to the selection of a course of action among several alternatives. Every _____ process produces a final choice. The output can be an action or an opinion of choice.
    a. 28-hour day
    b. 1990 Clean Air Act
    c. Decision making
    d. 33 Strategies of War

5. _____ is unwelcome harassment of a sexual nature, or based upon the receiving party's sex or gender. In some contexts or circumstances, _____ may be illegal. It includes a range of behavior from seemingly mild transgressions and annoyances to actual sexual abuse or sexual assault.

Chapter 4. Managerial Ethics and Corporate Social Responsibility

a. Hypernorms
b. 1990 Clean Air Act
c. 28-hour day
d. Sexual harassment

6. _____ consists of the mental process of thinking involved with the process of judging the merits of multiple options and selecting one of them for action. Some simple examples include deciding whether to get up in the morning or go back to sleep, or selecting a given route for a journey. More complex examples (often decisions that affect what a person thinks or their core beliefs) include choosing a lifestyle, religious affiliation, or political position.
   a. Groups decision making
   b. Trade study
   c. Choice
   d. Championship mobilization

7. _____ in its literal sense is the process of transformation of local or regional phenomena into global ones. It can be described as a process by which the people of the world are unified into a single society and function together.

This process is a combination of economic, technological, sociocultural and political forces.

   a. Histogram
   b. Globalization
   c. Collaborative Planning, Forecasting and Replenishment
   d. Cost Management

8. _____ is one of the managerial functions like planning, organizing, staffing and directing. It is an important function because it helps to check the errors and to take the corrective action so that deviation from standards are minimized and stated goals of the organization are achieved in desired manner. According to modern concepts, _____ is a foreseeing action whereas earlier concept of _____ was used only when errors were detected. _____ in management means setting standards, measuring actual performance and taking corrective action.
   a. Decision tree pruning
   b. Schedule of reinforcement
   c. Control
   d. Turnover

9. The United Nations _____ is an United Nations initiative to encourage businesses worldwide to adopt sustainable and socially responsible policies, and to report on their implementation. The _____ is a principle based framework for businesses, stating ten principles in the areas of human rights, labour, the environment and anti-corruption. Under the _____, companies are brought together with UN agencies, labour groups and civil society.

a. 1990 Clean Air Act
b. 33 Strategies of War
c. Global Compact
d. 28-hour day

10. Organizational culture is not the same as _____. It is wider and deeper concepts, something that an organization 'is' rather than what it 'has' (according to Buchanan and Huczynski.)

_____ is the total sum of the values, customs, traditions and meanings that make a company unique.

a. Path-goal theory
b. Corporate culture
c. Work design
d. Job analysis

11. A _____ is the belief that there is a technique, method, process, activity, incentive or reward that is more effective at delivering a particular outcome than any other technique, method, process, etc. The idea is that with proper processes, checks, and testing, a desired outcome can be delivered with fewer problems and unforeseen complications. _____s can also be defined as the most efficient (least amount of effort) and effective (best results) way of accomplishing a task, based on repeatable procedures that have proven themselves over time for large numbers of people.
a. Hierarchical organization
b. Design management
c. Fix it twice
d. Best practice

12. _____ occurs when a corporation is owned in whole or in part by its employees. Employees are usually given a share of the corporation after a certain length of employment or they can buy shares at any time. A corporation owned entirely by its employees (such as a worker cooperative) will not, therefore, have its shares sold on public stock markets, often opting instead for mixed ownership arrangements involving a trust.
a. Amoco Corporation
b. AT'T Inc.
c. Anaconda Copper
d. Employee ownership

13. _____ is the state or fact of exclusive rights and control over property, which may be an object, land/real estate or intellectual property. An _____ right is also referred to as title. The concept of _____ has existed for thousands of years and in all cultures.

a. Ownership
b. A4e
c. Emanation of the state
d. A Stake in the Outcome

14. In economics, _____ is a measure of the relative satisfaction from consumption of various goods and services. Given this measure, one may speak meaningfully of increasing or decreasing _____, and thereby explain economic behavior in terms of attempts to increase one's _____. For illustrative purposes, changes in _____ are sometimes expressed in units called utils.
   a. A Stake in the Outcome
   b. Indirect utility function
   c. Ordinal utility
   d. Utility

15. _____ has been described as the 'process of social influence in which one person can enlist the aid and support of others in the accomplishment of a common task' . A definition more inclusive of followers comes from Alan Keith of Genentech who said '_____ is ultimately about creating a way for people to contribute to making something extraordinary happen.'

_____ is one of the most salient aspects of the organizational context. However, defining _____ has been challenging.

   a. 28-hour day
   b. 1990 Clean Air Act
   c. Leadership
   d. Situational leadership

16. _____, e-commuting, e-work, telework, working from home (WFH), or working at home (WAH) is a work arrangement in which employees enjoy flexibility in working location and hours. In other words, the daily commute to a central place of work is replaced by telecommunication links. Many work from home, while others, occasionally also referred to as nomad workers or web commuters utilize mobile telecommunications technology to work from coffee shops or myriad other locations.
   a. 33 Strategies of War
   b. 28-hour day
   c. 1990 Clean Air Act
   d. Telecommuting

Chapter 5. Organizational Planning and Goal Setting

1. A _____ is a plan devised for a specific situation when things could go wrong. _____s are often devised by governments or businesses who want to be prepared for anything that could happen. They are sometimes known as 'Back-up plans', 'Worst-case scenario plans' or 'Plan B'.

    a. 33 Strategies of War
    b. 28-hour day
    c. Contingency plan
    d. 1990 Clean Air Act

2. A _____ is a brief written statement of the purpose of a company or organization. Ideally, a _____ guides the actions of the organization, spells out its overall goal, provides a sense of direction, and guides decision making for all levels of management.

    _____s often contain the following:

    - Purpose and aim of the organization
    - The organization's primary stakeholders: clients, stockholders, etc.
    - Responsibilities of the organization toward these stakeholders
    - Products and services offered

    In developing a _____:

    - Encourage as much input as feasible from employees, volunteers, and other stakeholders
    - Publicize it broadly

    The _____ can be used to resolve differences between business stakeholders. Stakeholders include: employees including managers and executives, stockholders, board of directors, customers, suppliers, distributors, creditors, governments (local, state, federal, etc.), unions, competitors, NGO's, and the general public.

    a. 1990 Clean Air Act
    b. Mission statement
    c. 33 Strategies of War
    d. 28-hour day

3. _____ can be regarded as an outcome of mental processes (cognitive process) leading to the selection of a course of action among several alternatives. Every _____ process produces a final choice. The output can be an action or an opinion of choice.

a. 28-hour day
b. 33 Strategies of War
c. 1990 Clean Air Act
d. Decision making

4. A _____ is the belief that there is a technique, method, process, activity, incentive or reward that is more effective at delivering a particular outcome than any other technique, method, process, etc. The idea is that with proper processes, checks, and testing, a desired outcome can be delivered with fewer problems and unforeseen complications. _____s can also be defined as the most efficient (least amount of effort) and effective (best results) way of accomplishing a task, based on repeatable procedures that have proven themselves over time for large numbers of people.

 a. Hierarchical organization
 b. Fix it twice
 c. Design management
 d. Best practice

5. _____ is a process of agreeing upon objectives within an organization so that management and employees agree to the objectives and understand what they are in the organization.

The term '_____' was first popularized by Peter Drucker in his 1954 book 'The Practice of Management'.

The essence of _____ is participative goal setting, choosing course of actions and decision making.

 a. Job enrichment
 b. Business economics
 c. Management by objectives
 d. Clean sheet review

6. _____ is the process by which an organization deals with any major unpredictable event that threatens to harm the organization, its stakeholders, or the general public. Three elements are common to most definitions of crisis: (a) a threat to the organization, (b) the element of surprise, and (c) a short decision time.

Whereas risk management involves assessing potential threats and finding the best ways to avoid those threats, _____ involves dealing with the disasters after they have occurred.

 a. Business value
 b. Capability management
 c. C-A-K-E
 d. Crisis management

Chapter 5. Organizational Planning and Goal Setting

7. _____ is generally a team of individuals at the highest level of organizational management who have the day-to-day responsibilities of managing a corporation. There are most often higher levels of responsibility, such as a board of directors and those who own the company (shareholders), but they focus on managing the _____ instead of the day-to-day activities of the business.

They are sometimes referred to, within corporations, as top management, upper management, higher management, or simply seniors.

    a. Senior management
    b. Management development
    c. Crisis management
    d. Functional management

8. In economics, business, retail, and accounting, a _____ is the value of money that has been used up to produce something, and hence is not available for use anymore. In economics, a _____ is an alternative that is given up as a result of a decision. In business, the _____ may be one of acquisition, in which case the amount of money expended to acquire it is counted as _____.

    a. Fixed costs
    b. Cost allocation
    c. Cost overrun
    d. Cost

9. _____ is a concept developed by Michael Porter, used in business strategy. It describes a way to establish the competitive advantage. _____, in basic words, means the lowest cost of operation in the industry.

    a. Strategic business unit
    b. Switching cost
    c. Strategic group
    d. Cost leadership

10. _____ has been described as the 'process of social influence in which one person can enlist the aid and support of others in the accomplishment of a common task'. A definition more inclusive of followers comes from Alan Keith of Genentech who said '_____ is ultimately about creating a way for people to contribute to making something extraordinary happen.'

_____ is one of the most salient aspects of the organizational context. However, defining _____ has been challenging.

a. 28-hour day
b. Leadership
c. 1990 Clean Air Act
d. Situational leadership

11. A _____ is a type of business entity in which partners (owners) share with each other the profits or losses of the business. _____s are often favored over corporations for taxation purposes, as the _____ structure does not generally incur a tax on profits before it is distributed to the partners (i.e. there is no dividend tax levied.) However, depending on the _____ structure and the jurisdiction in which it operates, owners of a _____ may be exposed to greater personal liability than they would as shareholders of a corporation.
    a. Federal Employers Liability Act
    b. Due process
    c. Mediation
    d. Partnership

12. _____ is an increasingly broadening term with which an organization, or other human system describes the combination of traditionally administrative personnel functions with acquisition and application of skills, knowledge and experience, Employee Relations and resource planning at various levels. The field draws upon concepts developed in Industrial/Organizational Psychology and System Theory. _____ has at least two related interpretations depending on context. The original usage derives from political economy and economics, where it was traditionally called labor, one of four factors of production although this perspective is changing as a function of new and ongoing research into more strategic approaches at national levels. This first usage is used more in terms of '_____ development', and can go beyond just organizations to the level of nations . The more traditional usage within corporations and businesses refers to the individuals within a firm or agency, and to the portion of the organization that deals with hiring, firing, training, and other personnel issues, typically referred to as `_____ management'.
    a. Progressive discipline
    b. Human Resources
    c. Bradford Factor
    d. Human resource management

Chapter 6. Managerial Decision Making

1. _____ can be regarded as an outcome of mental processes (cognitive process) leading to the selection of a course of action among several alternatives. Every _____ process produces a final choice. The output can be an action or an opinion of choice.
   a. 1990 Clean Air Act
   b. Decision making
   c. 33 Strategies of War
   d. 28-hour day

2. _____ of the learning curve effect and the closely related experience curve effect express the relationship between equations for experience and efficiency or between efficiency gains and investment in the effort. The experience of 'learning curves' was first observed by the 19th Century German psychologist Hermann Ebbinghaus according to the difficulty of memorizing varying numbers of verbal stimuli, and subsequent learning about the complex processes of learning are discussed in the

.

The rule used for representing the learning curve effect states that the more times a task has been performed, the less time will be required on each subsequent iteration.

   a. Point biserial correlation coefficient
   b. Spatial Decision Support Systems
   c. Distribution
   d. Models

3. _____ is a concept based on the fact that rationality of individuals is limited by the information they have, the cognitive limitations of their minds, and the finite amount of time they have to make decisions. This contrasts with the concept of rationality as optimization. Another way to look at _____ is that, because decision-makers lack the ability and resources to arrive at the optimal solution, they instead apply their rationality only after having greatly simplified the choices available.
   a. Transferable utility
   b. Mixed strategy
   c. Complete information
   d. Bounded rationality

4. A _____ is the belief that there is a technique, method, process, activity, incentive or reward that is more effective at delivering a particular outcome than any other technique, method, process, etc. The idea is that with proper processes, checks, and testing, a desired outcome can be delivered with fewer problems and unforeseen complications. _____s can also be defined as the most efficient (least amount of effort) and effective (best results) way of accomplishing a task, based on repeatable procedures that have proven themselves over time for large numbers of people.

Chapter 6. Managerial Decision Making 39

a. Hierarchical organization
b. Design management
c. Best practice
d. Fix it twice

5. A _____ is an alliance among individuals or groups, during which they cooperate in joint action, each in his own self-interest, joining forces together for a common cause. This alliance may be temporary or a matter of convenience. A _____ thus differs from a more formal covenant.
   a. 28-hour day
   b. 33 Strategies of War
   c. 1990 Clean Air Act
   d. Coalition

6. In decision theory and estimation theory, the _____ of an estimator, $\hat{\theta}$, of an unknown parameter of the distribution, θ, is the expected value of the loss function

$$R(\theta, \hat{\theta}) = \mathbb{E}_\theta L(\theta, \hat{\theta}) = \int L(\theta, \hat{\theta})\, dP_\theta.$$

Chapter 6. Managerial Decision Making

where dP_θ is a probability measure parametrized by θ.

- For a scalar parameter θ and a quadratic loss function,

$$L(\theta, \hat{\theta}) = (\theta - \hat{\theta})^2$$

the _____ function becomes the mean squared error of the estimate,

$$R(\theta, \hat{\theta}) = E_\theta (\theta - \hat{\theta})^2$$

- In density estimation, the unknown parameter is probability density itself. The loss function is typically chosen to be a norm in an appropriate function space. For example, for L^2 norm,

$$L(f, \hat{f}) = \|f - \hat{f}\|_2^2$$

the _____ function becomes the mean integrated squared error

$$R(f, \hat{f}) = E\|f - \hat{f}\|^2$$

a. Risk
b. Linear model
c. Risk aversion
d. Financial modeling

7. _____ has been described as the 'process of social influence in which one person can enlist the aid and support of others in the accomplishment of a common task'. A definition more inclusive of followers comes from Alan Keith of Genentech who said '_____ is ultimately about creating a way for people to contribute to making something extraordinary happen.'

_____ is one of the most salient aspects of the organizational context. However, defining _____ has been challenging.

a. 1990 Clean Air Act
b. Situational leadership
c. 28-hour day
d. Leadership

Chapter 6. Managerial Decision Making

8. _____, commonly referred to as 'eBusiness' or 'e-Business', may be defined as the utilization of information and communication technologies (ICT) in support of all the activities of business. Commerce constitutes the exchange of products and services between businesses, groups and individuals and hence can be seen as one of the essential activities of any business. Hence, electronic commerce or eCommerce focuses on the use of ICT to enable the external activities and relationships of the business with individuals, groups and other businesses .
   a. AAAI
   b. A Stake in the Outcome
   c. A4e
   d. Electronic business

9. The _____ is a job title for the board level head of information technology within an organization. The _____ typically reports to the chief operations officer or the chief executive officer. In military organizations, they report to the commanding officer or commanding general of the organization.
   a. 33 Strategies of War
   b. 1990 Clean Air Act
   c. 28-hour day
   d. Chief information officer

10. A _____ is a subset of the overall internal controls of a business covering the application of people, documents, technologies, and procedures by management accountants to solving business problems such as costing a product, service or a business-wide strategy. _____s are distinct from regular information systems in that they are used to analyze other information systems applied in operational activities in the organization. Academically, the term is commonly used to refer to the group of information management methods tied to the automation or support of human decision making, e.g. Decision Support Systems, Expert systems, and Executive information systems.
    a. 1990 Clean Air Act
    b. Strategic information system
    c. 28-hour day
    d. Management information system

11. _____ is the use of control systems (such as numerical control, programmable logic control, and other industrial control systems), in concert with other applications of information technology (such as computer-aided technologies [CAD, CAM, CAx]), to control industrial machinery and processes, reducing the need for human intervention. In the scope of industrialization, _____ is a step beyond mechanization. Whereas mechanization provided human operators with machinery to assist them with the physical requirements of work, _____ greatly reduces the need for human sensory and mental requirements as well.

a. A Stake in the Outcome
b. A4e
c. AAAI
d. Automation

12. _____, commonly known as e-commerce, consists of the buying and selling of products or services over electronic systems such as the Internet and other computer networks. The amount of trade conducted electronically has grown extraordinarily with widespread Internet usage. The use of commerce is conducted in this way, spurring and drawing on innovations in electronic funds transfer, supply chain management, Internet marketing, online transaction processing, electronic data interchange (EDI), inventory management systems, and automated data collection systems.
   a. Online shopping
   b. Electronic Commerce
   c. A Stake in the Outcome
   d. A4e

13. An _____ is a private network that uses Internet protocols, network connectivity, and possibly the public telecommunication system to securely share part of an organization's information or operations with suppliers, vendors, partners, customers or other businesses. An _____ can be viewed as part of a company's intranet that is extended to users outside the company (e.g.: normally over the Internet.) It has also been described as a 'state of mind' in which the Internet is perceived as a way to do business with a preapproved set of other companies business-to-business (B2B), in isolation from all other Internet users.
   a. A4e
   b. AAAI
   c. Extranet
   d. A Stake in the Outcome

14. An _____ is a private computer network that uses Internet technologies to securely share any part of an organization's information or operational systems with its employees. Sometimes the term refers only to the organization's internal website, but often it is a more extensive part of the organization's computer infrastructure and private websites are an important component and focal point of internal communication and collaboration.

An _____ is built from the same concepts and technologies used for the Internet, such as client-server computing and the Internet Protocol Suite (TCP/IP.)

   a. A4e
   b. AAAI
   c. A Stake in the Outcome
   d. Intranet

Chapter 6. Managerial Decision Making 43

15. _____ describes commerce transactions between businesses, such as between a manufacturer and a wholesaler, or between a wholesaler and a retailer. Contrasting terms are business-to-consumer (B2C) and business-to-government (B2G.)

The volume of B2B transactions is much higher than the volume of B2C transactions.

a. Market environment
b. Product bundling
c. Category management
d. Business-to-business

16. A _____ is a new organization or entity formed by a split from a larger one, such as a television series based on a pre-existing one, or a new company formed from a university research group or business incubator. In literature, especially in milieu-based popular fictional book series like mysteries, westerns, fantasy or science fiction, the term sub-series is generally used instead of _____, but with essentially the same meaning.

_____s as a descriptive term can also include a dissenting faction of a membership organization, a sect of a cult, or a denomination of a church.

a. 28-hour day
b. 33 Strategies of War
c. Spin-off
d. 1990 Clean Air Act

17. A _____ is the term given to a company that facilitates the learning of its members and continuously transforms itself. _____s develop as a result of the pressures facing modern organizations and enables them to remain competitive in the business environment. A _____ has five main features; systems thinking, personal mastery, mental models, shared vision and team learning.

a. Learning Organization
b. Quality function deployment
c. 1990 Clean Air Act
d. Hoshin Kanri

18. A _____ is a type of business entity in which partners (owners) share with each other the profits or losses of the business. _____s are often favored over corporations for taxation purposes, as the _____ structure does not generally incur a tax on profits before it is distributed to the partners (i.e. there is no dividend tax levied.) However, depending on the _____ structure and the jurisdiction in which it operates, owners of a _____ may be exposed to greater personal liability than they would as shareholders of a corporation.

Chapter 6. Managerial Decision Making

   a. Due process
   b. Partnership
   c. Mediation
   d. Federal Employers Liability Act

19. _____ is, in very basic words, a position a firm occupies against its competitors.

According to Michael Porter, the three methods for creating a sustainable _____ are through:

1. Cost leadership

2. Differentiation

3. Focus (economics)

   a. 1990 Clean Air Act
   b. Competitive advantage
   c. Theory Z
   d. 28-hour day

20. _____ is a recursive process where two or more people or organizations work together in an intersection of common goals -- for example, an intellectual endeavor that is creative in nature--by sharing knowledge, learning and building consensus. _____ does not require leadership and can sometimes bring better results through decentralization and egalitarianism. In particular, teams that work collaboratively can obtain greater resources, recognition and reward when facing competition for finite resources. _____ is also present in opposing goals exhibiting the notion of adversarial _____, though this is not a common case for using the term.
   a. 1990 Clean Air Act
   b. Collectivism
   c. Collaboration
   d. 28-hour day

21. _____ refers to increasing the spiritual, political, social or economic strength of individuals and communities. It often involves the empowered developing confidence in their own capacities.

The term Human _____ covers a vast landscape of meanings, interpretations, definitions and disciplines ranging from psychology and philosophy to the highly commercialized Self-Help industry and Motivational sciences.

Chapter 6. Managerial Decision Making

a. A4e
b. AAAI
c. A Stake in the Outcome
d. Empowerment

22. _____ is an area of knowledge within organizational theory that studies models and theories about the way an organization learns and adapts.

In Organizational development (OD), learning is a characteristic of an adaptive organization, i.e., an organization that is able to sense changes in signals from its environment (both internal and external) and adapt accordingly.

a. A4e
b. A Stake in the Outcome
c. AAAI
d. Organizational learning

Chapter 7. Fundamentals of Organizing

1. _____ is a structured approach to transitioning individuals, teams, and organizations from a current state to a desired future state. The current definition of _____ includes both organizational _____ processes and individual _____ models, which together are used to manage the people side of change.

A number of models are available for understanding the transitioning of individuals through the phases of _____ and strengthening organizational development initiative in both government and corporate sectors.

   a. Change management
   b. 33 Strategies of War
   c. 28-hour day
   d. 1990 Clean Air Act

2. An _____, or organogram(me)) is a diagram that shows the structure of an organization and the relationships and relative ranks of its parts and positions/jobs. The term is also used for similar diagrams, for example ones showing the different elements of a field of knowledge or a group of languages. The French Encyclopédie had one of the first _____s of knowledge in general.
   a. A Stake in the Outcome
   b. AAAI
   c. A4e
   d. Organizational chart

3. In a military context, the _____ is the line of authority and responsibility along which orders are passed within a military unit and between different units. The term is also used in a civilian management context describing comparable hierarchical structures of authority.
   a. 1990 Clean Air Act
   b. 28-hour day
   c. Chain of command
   d. French leave

4. The _____ is a standardized, on-scene, all-hazard incident management concept. It is a management protocol originally designed for emergency management agencies in the United States which was later federalized there. It has since been adopted by agencies in other countries.
   a. AAAI
   b. A4e
   c. A Stake in the Outcome
   d. Incident Command Structure

Chapter 7. Fundamentals of Organizing

5. _____ is a concept in ethics with several meanings. It is often used synonymously with such concepts as responsibility, answerability, enforcement, blameworthiness, liability and other terms associated with the expectation of account-giving. As an aspect of governance, it has been central to discussions related to problems in both the public and private (corporation) worlds.
   a. A4e
   b. Usury
   c. A Stake in the Outcome
   d. Accountability

6. _____ is the process by which the activities of an organisation, particularly those regarding decision-making, become concentrated within a particular location and/or group.
   a. Corner office
   b. Chief operating officer
   c. Product innovation
   d. Centralization

7. _____ is the process of dispersing decision-making governance closer to the people or citizen. It includes the dispersal of administration or governance in sectors or areas like engineering, management science, political science, political economy, sociology and economics. _____ is also possible in the dispersal of population and employment.
   a. Frenemy
   b. Business plan
   c. Formula for Change
   d. Decentralization

8. _____ refers to the process of grouping activities into departments.

Division of labour creates specialists who need coordination. This coordination is facilitated by grouping specialists together in departments.

   a. Maximum wage
   b. Departmentalization
   c. Division of labour
   d. Decent work

9. A _____ is a group of employees from various functional areas of the organization - research, engineering, marketing, finance. human resources, and operations, for example - who are all focused on a specific objective and are responsible to work as a team to improve coordination and innovation across divisions and resolve mutual problems.

a. Graduate recruitment
b. Cross-functional team
c. Sociotechnical systems
d. Goal-setting theory

10. A _____ is an organizational leader, responsible for ensuring that the organization maximizes the value it achieves through 'knowledge'. The _____ is responsible for managing intellectual capital and the custodian of Knowledge Management practices in an organization. _____ is not just a relabelling of the title 'chief information officer' - the _____ role is much broader.
a. Managing director
b. Chief knowledge officer
c. Hotel manager
d. General Manager

11. _____ refers to the movement of cash into or out of a business or financial product. It is usually measured during a specified, finite period of time. Measurement of _____ can be used

- to determine a project's rate of return or value. The time of _____s into and out of projects are used as inputs in financial models such as internal rate of return, and net present value.
- to determine problems with a business's liquidity. Being profitable does not necessarily mean being liquid. A company can fail because of a shortage of cash, even while profitable.
- as an alternate measure of a business's profits when it is believed that accrual accounting concepts do not represent economic realities. For example, a company may be notionally profitable but generating little operational cash (as may be the case for a company that barters its products rather than selling for cash.) In such a case, the company may be deriving additional operating cash by issuing shares evaluating default risk, re-investment requirements, etc.

_____ is a generic term used differently depending on the context. It may be defined by users for their own purposes.

a. Gross profit
b. Gross profit margin
c. Sweat equity
d. Cash flow

12. A _____ is a professional in the field of project management. _____s can have the responsibility of the planning, execution, and closing of any project, typically relating to construction industry, architecture, computer networking, telecommunications or software development.

Many other fields in the production, design and service industries also have _____s.

Chapter 7. Fundamentals of Organizing

a. Project management
b. Work package
c. Project manager
d. Project engineer

13. A _____ is the term given to a company that facilitates the learning of its members and continuously transforms itself. _____s develop as a result of the pressures facing modern organizations and enables them to remain competitive in the business environment. A _____ has five main features; systems thinking, personal mastery, mental models, shared vision and team learning.
   a. 1990 Clean Air Act
   b. Hoshin Kanri
   c. Quality function deployment
   d. Learning organization

14. _____ is a management technique pioneered by Michael Phillips in San Francisco in the late '60's and early '70s. The concept's most visible success was by Jack Stack and his team at SRC Holdings and popularized in 1995 by John Case. The technique is to give employees all relevant financial information about the company so they can make better decisions as workers.
   a. A4e
   b. AAAI
   c. A Stake in the Outcome
   d. Open-book management

15. _____ can be regarded as an outcome of mental processes (cognitive process) leading to the selection of a course of action among several alternatives. Every _____ process produces a final choice. The output can be an action or an opinion of choice.
   a. Decision making
   b. 28-hour day
   c. 33 Strategies of War
   d. 1990 Clean Air Act

16. _____ occurs when a corporation is owned in whole or in part by its employees. Employees are usually given a share of the corporation after a certain length of employment or they can buy shares at any time. A corporation owned entirely by its employees (such as a worker cooperative) will not, therefore, have its shares sold on public stock markets, often opting instead for mixed ownership arrangements involving a trust.

a. Amoco Corporation
b. Employee ownership
c. Anaconda Copper
d. AT'T Inc.

17. _____ refers to increasing the spiritual, political, social or economic strength of individuals and communities. It often involves the empowered developing confidence in their own capacities.

The term Human _____ covers a vast landscape of meanings, interpretations, definitions and disciplines ranging from psychology and philosophy to the highly commercialized Self-Help industry and Motivational sciences.

a. AAAI
b. A4e
c. A Stake in the Outcome
d. Empowerment

18. _____ is the state or fact of exclusive rights and control over property, which may be an object, land/real estate or intellectual property. An _____ right is also referred to as title. The concept of _____ has existed for thousands of years and in all cultures.
a. Emanation of the state
b. Ownership
c. A4e
d. A Stake in the Outcome

19. Organizational culture is not the same as _____. It is wider and deeper concepts, something that an organization 'is' rather than what it 'has' (according to Buchanan and Huczynski.)

_____ is the total sum of the values, customs, traditions and meanings that make a company unique.

a. Work design
b. Job analysis
c. Path-goal theory
d. Corporate culture

20. In economics, business, retail, and accounting, a _____ is the value of money that has been used up to produce something, and hence is not available for use anymore. In economics, a _____ is an alternative that is given up as a result of a decision. In business, the _____ may be one of acquisition, in which case the amount of money expended to acquire it is counted as _____.
a. Cost
b. Fixed costs
c. Cost allocation
d. Cost overrun

21. _____ is a concept developed by Michael Porter, used in business strategy. It describes a way to establish the competitive advantage. _____, in basic words, means the lowest cost of operation in the industry.
a. Strategic group
b. Switching cost
c. Strategic business unit
d. Cost leadership

22. _____ has been described as the 'process of social influence in which one person can enlist the aid and support of others in the accomplishment of a common task' . A definition more inclusive of followers comes from Alan Keith of Genentech who said '_____ is ultimately about creating a way for people to contribute to making something extraordinary happen.'

_____ is one of the most salient aspects of the organizational context. However, defining _____ has been challenging.

a. 1990 Clean Air Act
b. Situational leadership
c. 28-hour day
d. Leadership

23. _____ is a term originating in military organization theory, but now used more commonly in business management, particularly human resource management. _____ refers to the number of subordinates a supervisor has.

In the hierarchical business organization of the past it was not uncommon to see average spans of 1 to 10 or even less. That is, one manager supervised ten employees on average.

Chapter 7. Fundamentals of Organizing

a. Mentoring
b. CIFMS
c. Senior management
d. Span of control

24. _____ is one of the managerial functions like planning, organizing, staffing and directing. It is an important function because it helps to check the errors and to take the corrective action so that deviation from standards are minimized and stated goals of the organization are achieved in desired manner. According to modern concepts, _____ is a foreseeing action whereas earlier concept of _____ was used only when errors were detected. _____ in management means setting standards, measuring actual performance and taking corrective action.

a. Turnover
b. Schedule of reinforcement
c. Decision tree pruning
d. Control

25. In probability theory, a probability distribution is called _____ if its cumulative distribution function is _____. This is equivalent to saying that for random variables X with the distribution in question, Pr[X = a] = 0 for all real numbers a, i.e.: the probability that X attains the value a is zero, for any number a. If the distribution of X is _____ then X is called a _____ random variable.

a. Connectionist expert systems
b. Decision tree pruning
c. Pay Band
d. Continuous

26. _____ is the production of large amounts of standardized products, including and especially on assembly lines. The concepts of _____ are applied to various kinds of products, from fluids and particulates handled in bulk to discrete solid parts to assemblies of such parts

_____ of assemblies typically uses electric-motor-powered moving tracks or conveyor belts to move partially complete products to workers, who perform simple repetitive tasks.

a. 33 Strategies of War
b. 28-hour day
c. 1990 Clean Air Act
d. Mass production

Chapter 7. Fundamentals of Organizing

27. _____ is, according to the OED, 'the employment of cunning and duplicity in statecraft or in general conduct', deriving from the Italian Renaissance diplomat and writer Niccolò Machiavelli, who wrote Il Principe and other works. Machiavellian and variants became very popular in the late 16th century in English, though '_____' itself is first cited by the OED from 1626. The word has a similar use in modern psychology.
    a. Persuasion
    b. Self-enhancement
    c. Personal space
    d. Machiavellianism

28. _____, commonly referred to as 'eBusiness' or 'e-Business', may be defined as the utilization of information and communication technologies (ICT) in support of all the activities of business. Commerce constitutes the exchange of products and services between businesses, groups and individuals and hence can be seen as one of the essential activities of any business. Hence, electronic commerce or eCommerce focuses on the use of ICT to enable the external activities and relationships of the business with individuals, groups and other businesses .
    a. A4e
    b. AAAI
    c. A Stake in the Outcome
    d. Electronic business

Chapter 8. Change and Development

1. A _____ is the term given to a company that facilitates the learning of its members and continuously transforms itself. _____s develop as a result of the pressures facing modern organizations and enables them to remain competitive in the business environment. A _____ has five main features; systems thinking, personal mastery, mental models, shared vision and team learning.
   a. 1990 Clean Air Act
   b. Hoshin Kanri
   c. Quality function deployment
   d. Learning organization

2. _____ refers to increasing the spiritual, political, social or economic strength of individuals and communities. It often involves the empowered developing confidence in their own capacities.

   The term Human _____ covers a vast landscape of meanings, interpretations, definitions and disciplines ranging from psychology and philosophy to the highly commercialized Self-Help industry and Motivational sciences.

   a. Empowerment
   b. A Stake in the Outcome
   c. AAAI
   d. A4e

3. _____ is a structured approach to transitioning individuals, teams, and organizations from a current state to a desired future state. The current definition of _____ includes both organizational _____ processes and individual _____ models, which together are used to manage the people side of change.

   A number of models are available for understanding the transitioning of individuals through the phases of _____ and strengthening organizational development initiative in both government and corporate sectors.

   a. 28-hour day
   b. 33 Strategies of War
   c. 1990 Clean Air Act
   d. Change management

4. _____ is an inventory strategy that strives to improve the return on investment of a business by reducing in-process inventory and its associated carrying costs. To meet _____ objectives, the process relies on signals between different points in the process. This means the process is often driven by a series of signals, or Kanban , which tell production when to make the next part. Kanban are usually 'tickets' but can be simple visual signals, such as the presence or absence of a part on a shelf. Implemented correctly, _____ can dramatically improve a manufacturing organization's return on investment, quality, and efficiency.

Chapter 8. Change and Development 55

a. 28-hour day
b. Just-in-time
c. 33 Strategies of War
d. 1990 Clean Air Act

5. _____ is one of the managerial functions like planning, organizing, staffing and directing. It is an important function because it helps to check the errors and to take the corrective action so that deviation from standards are minimized and stated goals of the organization are achieved in desired manner. According to modern concepts, _____ is a foreseeing action whereas earlier concept of _____ was used only when errors were detected. _____ in management means setting standards, measuring actual performance and taking corrective action.
    a. Turnover
    b. Control
    c. Decision tree pruning
    d. Schedule of reinforcement

6. A _____ is the belief that there is a technique, method, process, activity, incentive or reward that is more effective at delivering a particular outcome than any other technique, method, process, etc. The idea is that with proper processes, checks, and testing, a desired outcome can be delivered with fewer problems and unforeseen complications. _____s can also be defined as the most efficient (least amount of effort) and effective (best results) way of accomplishing a task, based on repeatable procedures that have proven themselves over time for large numbers of people.
    a. Design management
    b. Fix it twice
    c. Hierarchical organization
    d. Best practice

7. The _____ captures an expanded spectrum of values and criteria for measuring organizational success: economic, ecological and social. With the ratification of the United Nations and ICLEI _____ standard for urban and community accounting in early 2007, this became the dominant approach to public sector full cost accounting. Similar UN standards apply to natural capital and human capital measurement to assist in measurements required by _____, e.g. the ecoBudget standard for reporting ecological footprint.
    a. 33 Strategies of War
    b. 1990 Clean Air Act
    c. 28-hour day
    d. Triple bottom line

8. In the field of human resource management, _____ is the field concerned with organizational activity aimed at bettering the performance of individuals and groups in organizational settings. It has been known by several names, including employee development, human resource development, and learning and development.

Harrison observes that the name was endlessly debated by the Chartered Institute of Personnel and Development during its review of professional standards in 1999/2000.

a. Person specification
b. Performance appraisal
c. Revolving door syndrome
d. Training and development

9. _____ refers to the long-term management of intractable conflicts. It is the label for the variety of ways by which people handle grievances--standing up for what they consider to be right and against what they consider to be wrong. Those ways include such diverse phenomena as gossip, ridicule, lynching, terrorism, warfare, feuding, genocide, law, mediation, and avoidance.

a. 1990 Clean Air Act
b. 33 Strategies of War
c. Conflict management
d. 28-hour day

10. The phrase _____ refers to the aspect of corporate strategy, corporate finance and management dealing with the buying, selling and combining of different companies that can aid, finance, or help a growing company in a given industry grow rapidly without having to create another business entity.

An acquisition, also known as a takeover or a buyout, is the buying of one company (the 'target') by another. An acquisition may be friendly or hostile.

a. Mergers and acquisitions
b. 33 Strategies of War
c. 28-hour day
d. 1990 Clean Air Act

11. As defined by Richard Beckhard, _____ is a planned, top-down, organization-wide effort to increase the organization's effectiveness and health. _____ is achieved through interventions in the organization's 'processes,' using behavioural science knowledge. According to Warren Bennis, _____ is a complex strategy intended to change the beliefs, attitudes, values, and structure of organizations so that they can better adapt to new technologies, markets, and challenges.

Chapter 8. Change and Development

a. Organizational structure
b. Organizational culture
c. Informal organization
d. Organizational Development

12. The phrase mergers and _____s refers to the aspect of corporate strategy, corporate finance and management dealing with the buying, selling and combining of different companies that can aid, finance, or help a growing company in a given industry grow rapidly without having to create another business entity.

An _____, also known as a takeover or a buyout, is the buying of one company (the 'target') by another. An _____ may be friendly or hostile.

a. Acquisition
b. A Stake in the Outcome
c. AAAI
d. A4e

13. _____ describes the situation when output from (or information about the result of) an event or phenomenon in the past will influence the same event/phenomenon in the present or future. When an event is part of a chain of cause-and-effect that forms a circuit or loop, then the event is said to 'feed back' into itself.

_____ is also a synonym for:

- _____ signal; the information about the initial event that is the basis for subsequent modification of the event.
- _____ loop; the causal path that leads from the initial generation of the _____ signal to the subsequent modification of the event.

_____ is a mechanism, process or signal that is looped back to control a system within itself. Such a loop is called a _____ loop.

a. 1990 Clean Air Act
b. Feedback
c. Feedback loop
d. Positive feedback

14. Organizational culture is not the same as _____. It is wider and deeper concepts, something that an organization 'is' rather than what it 'has' (according to Buchanan and Huczynski.)

_____ is the total sum of the values, customs, traditions and meanings that make a company unique.

a. Job analysis
b. Work design
c. Corporate culture
d. Path-goal theory

15. _____, commonly referred to as 'eBusiness' or 'e-Business', may be defined as the utilization of information and communication technologies (ICT) in support of all the activities of business. Commerce constitutes the exchange of products and services between businesses, groups and individuals and hence can be seen as one of the essential activities of any business. Hence, electronic commerce or eCommerce focuses on the use of ICT to enable the external activities and relationships of the business with individuals, groups and other businesses .

a. AAAI
b. A Stake in the Outcome
c. A4e
d. Electronic business

Chapter 9. Human Resource Management

1. _____ is the strategic and coherent approach to the management of an organisation's most valued assets - the people working there who individually and collectively contribute to the achievement of the objectives of the business. The terms '_____' and 'human resources' (HR) have largely replaced the term 'personnel management' as a description of the processes involved in managing people in organizations. In simple sense, _____ means employing people, developing their resources, utilizing, maintaining and compensating their services in tune with the job and organizational requirement.
   a. Progressive discipline
   b. Human resource management
   c. Job knowledge
   d. Revolving door syndrome

2. _____ is a form of corporate self-regulation integrated into a business model. Ideally, _____ policy would function as a built-in, self-regulating mechanism whereby business would monitor and ensure their adherence to law, ethical standards, and international norms. Business would embrace responsibility for the impact of their activities on the environment, consumers, employees, communities, stakeholders and all other members of the public sphere.
   a. 33 Strategies of War
   b. 1990 Clean Air Act
   c. 28-hour day
   d. Corporate social responsibility

3. In business and accounting, _____s are everything of value that is owned by a person or company. Any property or object of value that one possesses, usually considered as applicable to the payment of one's debts is considered an _____. Simplistically stated, _____s are things of value that can be readily converted into cash.
   a. A4e
   b. Asset
   c. AAAI
   d. A Stake in the Outcome

4. The _____ is the labour pool in employment. It is generally used to describe those working for a single company or industry, but can also apply to a geographic region like a city, country, state, etc. The term generally excludes the employers or management, and implies those involved in manual labour.
   a. Pink-collar worker
   b. Division of labour
   c. Workforce
   d. Work-life balance

5. _____ refers to the stock of skills and knowledge embodied in the ability to perform labor so as to produce economic value. It is the skills and knowledge gained by a worker through education and experience. Many early economic theories refer to it simply as labor, one of three factors of production, and consider it to be a fungible resource -- homogeneous and easily interchangeable.
   a. Deflation
   b. Market structure
   c. Productivity management
   d. Human capital

6. _____ in its literal sense is the process of transformation of local or regional phenomena into global ones. It can be described as a process by which the people of the world are unified into a single society and function together.

This process is a combination of economic, technological, sociocultural and political forces.

   a. Histogram
   b. Cost Management
   c. Collaborative Planning, Forecasting and Replenishment
   d. Globalization

7.

The terms _____ and positive action refer to policies that take race, ethnicity, or gender into consideration in an attempt to promote equal opportunity. The focus of such policies ranges from employment and education to public contracting and health programs. The impetus towards _____ is twofold: to maximize diversity in all levels of society, along with its presumed benefits, and to redress perceived disadvantages due to overt, institutional, or involuntary discrimination.

   a. Abraham Harold Maslow
   b. Adam Smith
   c. Affiliation
   d. Affirmative Action

8. _____ is a contract between two parties, one being the employer and the other being the employee. An employee may be defined as: 'A person in the service of another under any contract of hire, express or implied, oral or written, where the employer has the power or right to control and direct the employee in the material details of how the work is to be performed.' Black's Law Dictionary page 471 (5th ed. 1979.)

a. Exit interview
b. Employment
c. Employment counsellor
d. Employment rate

9. The term _____ was created by President Lyndon B. Johnson when he signed Executive Order 11246 on September 24, 1965, created to prohibit federal contractors from discriminating against employees on the basis of race, sex, creed, religion, color, or national origin. In more recent times, most employers have also added sexual orientation to the list of non-discrimination.

The Executive Order also required contractors to implement affirmative action plans to increase the participation of minorities and women in the workplace.

a. AAAI
b. A4e
c. A Stake in the Outcome
d. Equal Employment Opportunity

10. The U.S. _____ is a federal agency whose goal is ending employment discrimination. The _____ investigates discrimination complaints based on an individual's race, color, national origin, religion, sex, age, disability and retaliation for reporting and/or opposing a discriminatory practice. The Commission is also tasked with filing suits on behalf of alleged victim(s) of discrimination against employers and as an adjudicatory for claims of discrimination brought against federal agencies.

a. ARCO
b. Airbus Industrie
c. Airbus SAS
d. Equal Employment Opportunity Commission

11. _____ is unwelcome harassment of a sexual nature, or based upon the receiving party's sex or gender. In some contexts or circumstances, _____ may be illegal. It includes a range of behavior from seemingly mild transgressions and annoyances to actual sexual abuse or sexual assault.

a. 1990 Clean Air Act
b. 28-hour day
c. Hypernorms
d. Sexual harassment

12. _____ is a concept in ethics with several meanings. It is often used synonymously with such concepts as responsibility, answerability, enforcement, blameworthiness, liability and other terms associated with the expectation of account-giving. As an aspect of governance, it has been central to discussions related to problems in both the public and private (corporation) worlds.
   a. Usury
   b. A Stake in the Outcome
   c. A4e
   d. Accountability

13. _____ generally refers to a list of all planned expenses and revenues. It is a plan for saving and spending. A _____ is an important concept in microeconomics, which uses a _____ line to illustrate the trade-offs between two or more goods.
   a. Budget
   b. 28-hour day
   c. 1990 Clean Air Act
   d. 33 Strategies of War

14. The _____ of 1985 is a law passed by the U.S. Congress and signed by President Reagan that, among other things, mandates an insurance program giving some employees the ability to continue health insurance coverage after leaving employment. _____ includes amendments to the Employee Retirement Income Security Act of 1974 (ERISA.) The law deals with a great variety of subjects, such as tobacco price supports, railroads, private pension plans, disability insurance, and the postal service, but it is perhaps best known for Title X, which amends the Internal Revenue Code to deny income tax deductions to employers for contributions to a group health plan unless such plan meets certain continuing coverage requirements.
   a. 28-hour day
   b. 1990 Clean Air Act
   c. 33 Strategies of War
   d. Consolidated Omnibus Budget Reconciliation Act

15. _____ is a cross-disciplinary area concerned with protecting the safety, health and welfare of people engaged in work or employment. The goal of all _____ programs is to foster a work free safe environment. As a secondary effect, it may also protect co-workers, family members, employers, customers, suppliers, nearby communities, and other members of the public who are impacted by the workplace environment.
   a. Occupational Safety and Health
   b. A Stake in the Outcome
   c. A4e
   d. AAAI

Chapter 9. Human Resource Management

16. The _____ is the primary federal law which governs occupational health and safety in the private sector and federal government in the United States. It was enacted by Congress in 1970 and was signed by President Richard Nixon on December 29, 1970. Its main goal is to ensure that employers provide employees with an environment free from recognized hazards, such as exposure to toxic chemicals, excessive noise levels, mechanical dangers, heat or cold stress, or unsanitary conditions.

   a. Unemployment and Farm Relief Act
   b. Unemployment Action Center
   c. Occupational Safety and Health Act
   d. United States Department of Justice

17. The U.S. _____ of 1973 prohibits discrimination on the basis of disability in programs conducted by Federal agencies, in programs receiving Federal financial assistance, in Federal employment, and in the employment practices of Federal contractors. The standards for determining employment discrimination under the _____ are the same as those used in title I of the Americans with Disabilities Act.

There are four key sections of the Act.

   a. 28-hour day
   b. 33 Strategies of War
   c. 1990 Clean Air Act
   d. Rehabilitation Act

18. _____ is a term defined by the Oxford English Dictionary as an individual's 'course or progress through life '. It is usually considered to pertain to remunerative work (and sometimes also formal education.)

The etymology of the term is somewhat ironic in that it comes from the Latin word carrera, which means race .

   a. Spatial mismatch
   b. Career
   c. Career planning
   d. Nursing shortage

19. The 'business case for _____', theorizes that in a global marketplace, a company that employs a diverse workforce (both men and women, people of many generations, people from ethnically and racially diverse backgrounds etc.) is better able to understand the demographics of the marketplace it serves and is thus better equipped to thrive in that marketplace than a company that has a more limited range of employee demographics.

An additional corollary suggests that a company that supports the _____ of its workforce can also improve employee satisfaction, productivity and retention.

a. Trademark
b. Diversity
c. Virtual team
d. Kanban

20. _____, e-commuting, e-work, telework, working from home (WFH), or working at home (WAH) is a work arrangement in which employees enjoy flexibility in working location and hours. In other words, the daily commute to a central place of work is replaced by telecommunication links. Many work from home, while others, occasionally also referred to as nomad workers or web commuters utilize mobile telecommunications technology to work from coffee shops or myriad other locations.
a. 28-hour day
b. 1990 Clean Air Act
c. 33 Strategies of War
d. Telecommuting

21. _____ refers to the movement of cash into or out of a business or financial product. It is usually measured during a specified, finite period of time. Measurement of _____ can be used

- to determine a project's rate of return or value. The time of _____s into and out of projects are used as inputs in financial models such as internal rate of return, and net present value.
- to determine problems with a business's liquidity. Being profitable does not necessarily mean being liquid. A company can fail because of a shortage of cash, even while profitable.
- as an alternate measure of a business's profits when it is believed that accrual accounting concepts do not represent economic realities. For example, a company may be notionally profitable but generating little operational cash (as may be the case for a company that barters its products rather than selling for cash.) In such a case, the company may be deriving additional operating cash by issuing shares evaluating default risk, re-investment requirements, etc.

_____ is a generic term used differently depending on the context. It may be defined by users for their own purposes.

a. Sweat equity
b. Gross profit margin
c. Cash flow
d. Gross profit

22. _____ is the discipline of planning, organizing and managing resources to bring about the successful completion of specific project goals and objectives. It is often closely related to and sometimes conflated with Program management.

A project is a finite endeavor--having specific start and completion dates--undertaken to meet particular goals and objectives, usually to bring about beneficial change or added value.

a. Work package
b. Precedence diagram
c. Project engineer
d. Project management

23. _____ is an increasingly broadening term with which an organization, or other human system describes the combination of traditionally administrative personnel functions with acquisition and application of skills, knowledge and experience, Employee Relations and resource planning at various levels. The field draws upon concepts developed in Industrial/Organizational Psychology and System Theory. _____ has at least two related interpretations depending on context. The original usage derives from political economy and economics, where it was traditionally called labor, one of four factors of production although this perspective is changing as a function of new and ongoing research into more strategic approaches at national levels. This first usage is used more in terms of '_____ development', and can go beyond just organizations to the level of nations . The more traditional usage within corporations and businesses refers to the individuals within a firm or agency, and to the portion of the organization that deals with hiring, firing, training, and other personnel issues, typically referred to as `_____ management'.
   a. Progressive discipline
   b. Bradford Factor
   c. Human resource management
   d. Human resources

24. In macroeconomics, _____ is a mathematical framework describing the formation of mutually beneficial relationships over time. It offers a way of modeling markets in which frictions prevent instantaneous adjustment of the level of economic activity. Among other applications, it has been used as a framework for studying frictional unemployment.
   a. Control
   b. Pay Band
   c. Center for Group Studies
   d. Matching theory

25. _____ refers to various methodologies for analyzing the requirements of a job.

The general purpose of _____ is to document the requirements of a job and the work performed. Job and task analysis is performed as a basis for later improvements, including: definition of a job domain; describing a job; developing performance appraisals, selection systems, promotion criteria, training needs assessment, and compensation plans.

a. Work design
b. Hersey-Blanchard situational theory
c. Management process
d. Job analysis

26. A _____ is a list of the general tasks and responsibilities of a position. Typically, it also includes to whom the position reports, specifications such as the qualifications needed by the person in the job, salary range for the position, etc. A _____ is usually developed by conducting a job analysis, which includes examining the tasks and sequences of tasks necessary to perform the job.
    a. Recruitment advertising
    b. Recruitment
    c. Recruitment Process Insourcing
    d. Job description

27. The term _____ in logic applies to arguments or statements.

An argument is valid if and only if the truth of its premises entails the truth of its conclusion, it would be self-contradictory to affirm the premises and deny the conclusion. The corresponding conditional of a valid argument is a logical truth and the negation of its corresponding conditional is a contradiction.

   a. 1990 Clean Air Act
   b. Validity
   c. Fuzzy logic
   d. Simplification

28. _____ is a property of a test intended to measure something. The test is said to have _____ if it 'looks like' it is going to measure what it is supposed to measure. For instance, if you prepare a test to measure whether students can perform multiplication, and the people you show it to all agree that it looks like a good test of multiplication ability, you have shown the _____ of your test.
    a. Face validity
    b. 33 Strategies of War
    c. 1990 Clean Air Act
    d. 28-hour day

29. _____ refers to training in different ways to improve overall performance. It takes advantage of the particular effectiveness of each training method, while at the same time attempting to neglect the shortcomings of that method by combining it with other methods that address its weaknesses.

Cross training is employee-employer field means, training employees to do one another's work.

a. 28-hour day
b. Cross-training
c. 33 Strategies of War
d. 1990 Clean Air Act

30. In the field of human resource management, _____ is the field concerned with organizational activity aimed at bettering the performance of individuals and groups in organizational settings. It has been known by several names, including employee development, human resource development, and learning and development.

Harrison observes that the name was endlessly debated by the Chartered Institute of Personnel and Development during its review of professional standards in 1999/2000.

a. Performance appraisal
b. Person specification
c. Training and development
d. Revolving door syndrome

31. In economics, business, retail, and accounting, a _____ is the value of money that has been used up to produce something, and hence is not available for use anymore. In economics, a _____ is an alternative that is given up as a result of a decision. In business, the _____ may be one of acquisition, in which case the amount of money expended to acquire it is counted as _____.

a. Fixed costs
b. Cost allocation
c. Cost
d. Cost overrun

32. A _____ is the belief that there is a technique, method, process, activity, incentive or reward that is more effective at delivering a particular outcome than any other technique, method, process, etc. The idea is that with proper processes, checks, and testing, a desired outcome can be delivered with fewer problems and unforeseen complications. _____s can also be defined as the most efficient (least amount of effort) and effective (best results) way of accomplishing a task, based on repeatable procedures that have proven themselves over time for large numbers of people.

a. Hierarchical organization
b. Fix it twice
c. Best practice
d. Design management

Chapter 9. Human Resource Management

33. In human resources or industrial/organizational psychology, _____' 'multisource feedback,' or 'multisource assessment,' is feedback that comes from all around an employee. '360' refers to the 360 degrees in a circle, with an individual figuratively in the center of the circle. Feedback is provided by subordinates, peers, and supervisors.
    a. Job knowledge
    b. Personnel management
    c. Revolving door syndrome
    d. 360-degree feedback

34. _____ describes the situation when output from (or information about the result of) an event or phenomenon in the past will influence the same event/phenomenon in the present or future. When an event is part of a chain of cause-and-effect that forms a circuit or loop, then the event is said to 'feed back' into itself.

    _____ is also a synonym for:

    - _____ signal; the information about the initial event that is the basis for subsequent modification of the event.
    - _____ loop; the causal path that leads from the initial generation of the _____ signal to the subsequent modification of the event.

    _____ is a mechanism, process or signal that is looped back to control a system within itself. Such a loop is called a _____ loop.

    a. Feedback
    b. Feedback loop
    c. 1990 Clean Air Act
    d. Positive feedback

35. _____ is a method by which the job performance of an employee is evaluated _____ is a part of career development.

    _____s are regular reviews of employee performance within organizations

Generally, the aims of a _____ are to:

- Give feedback on performance to employees.
- Identify employee training needs.
- Document criteria used to allocate organizational rewards.
- Form a basis for personnel decisions: salary increases, promotions, disciplinary actions, etc.
- Provide the opportunity for organizational diagnosis and development.
- Facilitate communication between employee and administraton
- Validate selection techniques and human resource policies to meet federal Equal Employment Opportunity requirements.

A common approach to assessing performance is to use a numerical or scalar rating system whereby managers are asked to score an individual against a number of objectives/attributes. In some companies, employees receive assessments from their manager, peers, subordinates and customers while also performing a self assessment.

a. Personnel management
b. Human resource management
c. Progressive discipline
d. Performance appraisal

36. The _____ refers to a cognitive bias whereby the perception of a particular trait is influenced by the perception of the former traits in a sequence of interpretations.

Edward L. Thorndike was the first to support the _____ with empirical research. In a psychology study published in 1920, Thorndike asked commanding officers to rate their soldiers; Thorndike found high cross-correlation between all positive and all negative traits.

a. Halo effect
b. Cognitive biases
c. Sunk costs
d. Distinction bias

37. A _____ is a set of categories designed to elicit information about a quantitative or a qualitative attribute. In the social sciences, common examples are the Likert scale and 1-10 _____s in which a person selects the number which is considered to reflect the perceived quality of a product.

A _____ is an instrument that requires the rater to assign the rated object that have numerals assigned to them.

Chapter 9. Human Resource Management

   a. Rating scale
   b. Spearman-Brown prediction formula
   c. Thurstone scale
   d. Polytomous Rasch model

38. A _____ is a compensation, usually financial, received by a worker in exchange for their labor.

Compensation in terms of _____s is given to worker and compensation in terms of salary is given to employees. Compensation is a monetary benefits given to employees in returns of the services provided by them.

   a. Performance-related pay
   b. Profit-sharing agreement
   c. State Compensation Insurance Fund
   d. Wage

39. A _____ is a form of periodic payment from an employer to an employee, which may be specified in an employment contract. It is contrasted with piece wages, where each job, hour or other unit is paid separately, rather than on a periodic basis.

From the point of a view of running a business, _____ can also be viewed as the cost of acquiring human resources for running operations, and is then termed personnel expense or _____ expense.

   a. Human resource management
   b. Human resources
   c. Training and development
   d. Salary

40. _____ is the process of systematically determining a relative value of jobs in an organisation. In all cases the idea is to evaluate the job, not the person doing it.

- Job Ranking is the most simple form. Basically you just order the jobs according to perceived seniority. It's easy in a small organization, but get exponentially difficult with lots of different jobs.

- Pair Comparison introduces more rigour by comparing jobs in pairs, but really it's a more structured way of building a basic rank order.

- Benchmarking or slotting sets up certain jobs that are analysed in detail. These are then used for comparison to slot jobs against these benchmarks.

a. Job evaluation
b. 33 Strategies of War
c. 1990 Clean Air Act
d. 28-hour day

41. An _____ is an interview conducted by an employer of a departing employee. They are generally conducted by a relatively neutral party, such as a human resources staff member, so that the employee will be more inclined to be candid, as opposed to worrying about burning bridges. For this reason, some companies opt to employ a third party to conduct the interviews and provide feedback.
   a. Occupational Employment Statistics
   b. Underemployment
   c. Extra role performance
   d. Exit interview

42. The _____ is a United States labor law allowing an employee to take unpaid leave due to a serious health condition that makes the employee unable to perform his job or to care for a sick family member or to care for a new son or daughter (including by birth, adoption or foster care.) The bill was among the first signed into law by President Bill Clinton in his first term.
   a. Contributory negligence
   b. Harvester Judgment
   c. Family and Medical Leave Act of 1993
   d. Sarbanes-Oxley Act of 2002

43. The phrase _____ refers to the aspect of corporate strategy, corporate finance and management dealing with the buying, selling and combining of different companies that can aid, finance, or help a growing company in a given industry grow rapidly without having to create another business entity.

An acquisition, also known as a takeover or a buyout, is the buying of one company (the 'target') by another. An acquisition may be friendly or hostile.

   a. 28-hour day
   b. 33 Strategies of War
   c. 1990 Clean Air Act
   d. Mergers and acquisitions

Chapter 9. Human Resource Management

44. _____ occurs when a person is available to work and seeking work but currently without work. The prevalence of _____ is usually measured using the _____ rate, which is defined as the percentage of those in the labor force who are unemployed. The _____ rate is also used in economic studies and economic indexes such as the United States' Conference Board's Index of Leading Indicators as a measure of the state of the macroeconomics.
   a. Employment-to-population ratio
   b. Unemployment Convention, 1919
   c. Unemployment
   d. Outplacement

45. _____ is money received by an unemployed worker from the United States or a state. In the United States, this compensation is classified as a type of social welfare benefit. According to the Internal Revenue Code, these types of benefits are to be included in a taxpayer's gross income.
   a. Unemployment Provision Convention, 1934
   b. Unemployment
   c. Unemployment compensation
   d. Unemployment insurance

46. The phrase mergers and _____s refers to the aspect of corporate strategy, corporate finance and management dealing with the buying, selling and combining of different companies that can aid, finance, or help a growing company in a given industry grow rapidly without having to create another business entity.

An _____, also known as a takeover or a buyout, is the buying of one company (the 'target') by another. An _____ may be friendly or hostile.

   a. A Stake in the Outcome
   b. AAAI
   c. A4e
   d. Acquisition

47. _____ is the temporary suspension or permanent termination of employment of an employee or (more commonly) a group of employees for business reasons, such as the decision that certain positions are no longer necessary or a business slow-down or interruption in work. Originally the term '_____' referred exclusively to a temporary interruption in work, as when factory work cyclically falls off. However, in recent times the term can also refer to the permanent elimination of a position.
   a. Termination of employment
   b. Wrongful dismissal
   c. Retirement
   d. Layoff

Chapter 10. Managing Diverse Employees

1. The 'business case for _____', theorizes that in a global marketplace, a company that employs a diverse workforce (both men and women, people of many generations, people from ethnically and racially diverse backgrounds etc.) is better able to understand the demographics of the marketplace it serves and is thus better equipped to thrive in that marketplace than a company that has a more limited range of employee demographics.

An additional corollary suggests that a company that supports the _____ of its workforce can also improve employee satisfaction, productivity and retention.

   a. Diversity
   b. Virtual team
   c. Kanban
   d. Trademark

2. _____ is the strategic and coherent approach to the management of an organisation's most valued assets - the people working there who individually and collectively contribute to the achievement of the objectives of the business. The terms '_____' and 'human resources' (HR) have largely replaced the term 'personnel management' as a description of the processes involved in managing people in organizations. In simple sense, _____ means employing people, developing their resources, utilizing, maintaining and compensating their services in tune with the job and organizational requirement.
   a. Progressive discipline
   b. Job knowledge
   c. Revolving door syndrome
   d. Human Resource Management

3. The _____ is the labour pool in employment. It is generally used to describe those working for a single company or industry, but can also apply to a geographic region like a city, country, state, etc. The term generally excludes the employers or management, and implies those involved in manual labour.
   a. Pink-collar worker
   b. Division of labour
   c. Work-life balance
   d. Workforce

4. _____ is the statistical study of all populations. It can be a very general science that can be applied to any kind of dynamic population, that is, one that changes over time or space It encompasses the study of the size, structure and distribution of populations, and spatial and/or temporal changes in them in response to birth, migration, aging and death.
   a. 33 Strategies of War
   b. 1990 Clean Air Act
   c. 28-hour day
   d. Demography

Chapter 10. Managing Diverse Employees

5. _____ or _____ data refers to selected population characteristics as used in government, marketing or opinion research, or the _____ profiles used in such research. Note the distinction from the term 'demography' Commonly-used _____s include race, age, income, disabilities, mobility (in terms of travel time to work or number of vehicles available), educational attainment, home ownership, employment status, and even location.
   a. Adam Smith
   b. Abraham Harold Maslow
   c. Affiliation
   d. Demographic

6.

The terms _____ and positive action refer to policies that take race, ethnicity, or gender into consideration in an attempt to promote equal opportunity. The focus of such policies ranges from employment and education to public contracting and health programs. The impetus towards _____ is twofold: to maximize diversity in all levels of society, along with its presumed benefits, and to redress perceived disadvantages due to overt, institutional, or involuntary discrimination.

   a. Affiliation
   b. Affirmative action
   c. Abraham Harold Maslow
   d. Adam Smith

7. A policy of _____ is typically adopted in nations that have emerged from a history of national or ethnic conflict in which neither side has gained complete victory. This condition usually arises as a consequence of colonial settlement. The resulting conflict may be either between colonisers and indigenous people or between rival groups of colonisers.
   a. 1990 Clean Air Act
   b. 28-hour day
   c. 33 Strategies of War
   d. Biculturalism

8. In economics, the term _____ refers to situations where the advancement of a qualified person within the hierarchy of an organization is stopped at a lower level because of some form of discrimination, most commonly sexism or racism, but since the term was coined, '_____' has also come to describe the limited advancement of the deaf, blind, disabled, aged and sexual minorities.It is an unofficial, invisible barrier that prevents women and minorities from advancing in businesses.

Chapter 10. Managing Diverse Employees

This situation is referred to as a 'ceiling' as there is a limitation blocking upward advancement, and 'glass' (transparent) because the limitation is not immediately apparent and is normally an unwritten and unofficial policy. This invisible barrier continues to exist, even though there are no explicit obstacles keeping minorities from acquiring advanced job positions - there are no advertisements that specifically say 'no minorities hired at this establishment', nor are there any formal orders that say 'minorities are not qualified' - but they do lie beneath the surface.

   a. 1990 Clean Air Act
   b. 28-hour day
   c. 33 Strategies of War
   d. Glass ceiling

9. _____ is a term used to describe the lifestyle of women who choose to leave the workforce (typically in white collar career positions) in order to pursue childbearing. This is the converse of the Fast Track, where one devotes considerable energy to career building.

This is a source of considerable political and social discussion.

   a. 1990 Clean Air Act
   b. 28-hour day
   c. 33 Strategies of War
   d. Mommy track

10. A _____ is a compensation, usually financial, received by a worker in exchange for their labor.

Compensation in terms of _____s is given to worker and compensation in terms of salary is given to employees. Compensation is a monetary benefits given to employees in returns of the services provided by them.

   a. Performance-related pay
   b. State Compensation Insurance Fund
   c. Profit-sharing agreement
   d. Wage

11. Income disparity or _____ is a term used to describe inequities and asymmetry in the distribution of wealth and income between socio-economic groups within society. The term also has many other definitions:

Common examples include:

- The income gap between the wealthy and the poor.
- lower average income for females than males

In the context of economic inequality, gender gap generally refers to the differences in the wages of men and women, or boys and girls. There is a debate to what extent this is the result of gender differences, lifestyle choices (e.g., number of hours worked), or because of discrimination.

A United Nations report found that women working in manufacturing earned the following percentages in relation to men in 2003.

a. Workforce
b. Quality of working life
c. Division of labour
d. Wage gap

12. The _____ is a United States statute that was passed in response to a series of United States Supreme Court decisions which limited the rights of employees who had sued their employers for discrimination. The Act represented the first effort since the passage of the Civil Rights Act of 1964 to modify some of the basic procedural and substantive rights provided by federal law in employment discrimination cases. It provided for the right to trial by jury on discrimination claims and introduced the possibility of emotional distress damages, while limiting the amount that a jury could award

The 1991 Act combined elements from two different civil rights acts of the past: the Civil Rights Act of 1866, better known by the number assigned to it in the codification of federal laws as 'Section 1981', and the employment-related provisions of the Civil Rights Act of 1964, generally referred to as 'Title VII', its location within the Act.

a. Negligence in employment
b. Covenant
c. Resource Conservation and Recovery Act
d. Civil Rights Act of 1991

13. An _____ is a person who has possession of an enterprise and assumes significant accountability for the inherent risks and the outcome. It is an ambitious leader who combines land, labor, and capital to create and market new goods or services. The term is a loanword from French and was first defined by the Irish economist Richard Cantillon.

a. A Stake in the Outcome
b. AAAI
c. A4e
d. Entrepreneur

14. Organizational culture is not the same as _____. It is wider and deeper concepts, something that an organization 'is' rather than what it 'has' (according to Buchanan and Huczynski.)

_____ is the total sum of the values, customs, traditions and meanings that make a company unique.

a. Path-goal theory
b. Work design
c. Job analysis
d. Corporate culture

15. _____ is unwelcome harassment of a sexual nature, or based upon the receiving party's sex or gender. In some contexts or circumstances, _____ may be illegal. It includes a range of behavior from seemingly mild transgressions and annoyances to actual sexual abuse or sexual assault.
a. 28-hour day
b. 1990 Clean Air Act
c. Hypernorms
d. Sexual harassment

16. _____ has been described as the 'process of social influence in which one person can enlist the aid and support of others in the accomplishment of a common task' . A definition more inclusive of followers comes from Alan Keith of Genentech who said '_____ is ultimately about creating a way for people to contribute to making something extraordinary happen.'

_____ is one of the most salient aspects of the organizational context. However, defining _____ has been challenging.

a. 28-hour day
b. Leadership
c. Situational leadership
d. 1990 Clean Air Act

17. _____ is a term defined by the Oxford English Dictionary as an individual's 'course or progress through life '. It is usually considered to pertain to remunerative work (and sometimes also formal education.)

The etymology of the term is somewhat ironic in that it comes from the Latin word carrera, which means race .

a. Spatial mismatch
b. Career planning
c. Career
d. Nursing shortage

18. _____ refers to the process of screening, and selecting qualified people for a job at an organization or firm mid- and large-size organizations and companies often retain professional recruiters or outsource some of the process to _____ agencies. External _____ is the process of attracting and selecting employees from outside the organization.

The _____ industry has four main types of agencies: employment agencies, _____ websites and job search engines, 'headhunters' for executive and professional _____, and in-house _____.

a. Recruitment Process Outsourcing
b. Referral recruitment
c. Labour hire
d. Recruitment

19. _____, commonly abbreviated to Gen X, is a term used to refer to a generational cohort of children born after the baby boom ended and usually prior to the 1980s

The term _____ has been used in demography, the social sciences, and marketing, though it is most often used in popular culture.

In the U.S. _____ was originally referred to as the 'baby bust' generation because of the drop in the birth rate following the baby boom.

a. Affiliation
b. Abraham Harold Maslow
c. Adam Smith
d. Generation X

20. _____ is a term used to describe the demographic cohort following Generation X. Its members are often referred to as 'Millennials' or 'Echo Boomers') . There are no precise dates for when Gen Y begins and ends. Most commentators use dates from the early 1980s to early 1990s.

a. Benjamin R. Barber
b. David Wittig
c. Giovanni Agnelli
d. Generation Y

21. There are two types of _____ relationships: formal and informal. Informal relationships develop on their own between partners. Formal _____, on the other hand, refers to assigned relationships, often associated with organizational _____ programs designed to promote employee development or to assist at-risk children and youth.
   a. Real Property Administrator
   b. Fix it twice
   c. Human resource management system
   d. Mentoring

22. An _____ is a person temporarily or permanently residing in a country and culture other than that of the person's upbringing or legal residence. The word comes from the Latin ex and patria (country, fatherland.)

The term is sometimes used in the context of Westerners living in non-Western countries, although it is also used to describe Westerners living in other Western countries, such as Americans living in the United Kingdom, or Britons living in Spain.

   a. AAAI
   b. Expatriate
   c. A Stake in the Outcome
   d. A4e

23. _____ in its literal sense is the process of transformation of local or regional phenomena into global ones. It can be described as a process by which the people of the world are unified into a single society and function together.

This process is a combination of economic, technological, sociocultural and political forces.

   a. Histogram
   b. Collaborative Planning, Forecasting and Replenishment
   c. Globalization
   d. Cost Management

24. In business and accounting, _____s are everything of value that is owned by a person or company. Any property or object of value that one possesses, usually considered as applicable to the payment of one's debts is considered an _____. Simplistically stated, _____s are things of value that can be readily converted into cash.

a. AAAI
b. A4e
c. A Stake in the Outcome
d. Asset

25. _____ is a contract between two parties, one being the employer and the other being the employee. An employee may be defined as: 'A person in the service of another under any contract of hire, express or implied, oral or written, where the employer has the power or right to control and direct the employee in the material details of how the work is to be performed.' Black's Law Dictionary page 471 (5th ed. 1979.)
    a. Employment rate
    b. Employment counsellor
    c. Exit interview
    d. Employment

Chapter 11. Foundations of Behavior in Organizations

1. _____ is a form of communication that typically attempts to persuade potential customers to purchase or to consume more of a particular brand of product or service. 'While now central to the contemporary global economy and the reproduction of global production networks, it is only quite recently that _____ has been more than a marginal influence on patterns of sales and production. The formation of modern _____ was intimately bound up with the emergence of new forms of monopoly capitalism around the end of the 19th and beginning of the 20th century as one element in corporate strategies to create, organize and where possible control markets, especially for mass produced consumer goods.
   a. Advertising
   b. AAAI
   c. A4e
   d. A Stake in the Outcome

2. _____ describes commerce transactions between businesses, such as between a manufacturer and a wholesaler, or between a wholesaler and a retailer. Contrasting terms are business-to-consumer (B2C) and business-to-government (B2G.)

   The volume of B2B transactions is much higher than the volume of B2C transactions.

   a. Category management
   b. Business-to-business
   c. Market environment
   d. Product bundling

3. _____ has been described as the 'process of social influence in which one person can enlist the aid and support of others in the accomplishment of a common task' . A definition more inclusive of followers comes from Alan Keith of Genentech who said '_____ is ultimately about creating a way for people to contribute to making something extraordinary happen.'

   _____ is one of the most salient aspects of the organizational context. However, defining _____ has been challenging.

   a. Situational leadership
   b. Leadership
   c. 28-hour day
   d. 1990 Clean Air Act

4. _____, commonly known as e-commerce, consists of the buying and selling of products or services over electronic systems such as the Internet and other computer networks. The amount of trade conducted electronically has grown extraordinarily with widespread Internet usage. The use of commerce is conducted in this way, spurring and drawing on innovations in electronic funds transfer, supply chain management, Internet marketing, online transaction processing, electronic data interchange (EDI), inventory management systems, and automated data collection systems.

a. A4e
b. Online shopping
c. Electronic Commerce
d. A Stake in the Outcome

5. _____ describes how content an individual is with his or her job.

The happier people are within their job, the more satisfied they are said to be. _____ is not the same as motivation, although it is clearly linked.

a. Job satisfaction
b. Human relations
c. Goal-setting theory
d. Job analysis

6. _____ is an uncomfortable feeling caused by holding two contradictory ideas simultaneously. The 'ideas' or 'cognitions' in question may include attitudes and beliefs, and also the awareness of one's behavior. The theory of _____ proposes that people have a motivational drive to reduce dissonance by changing their attitudes, beliefs, and behaviors, or by justifying or rationalizing their attitudes, beliefs, and behaviors.

a. Quantitative psychology
b. Cognitive dissonance
c. Trait theory
d. Cognitive bias

7. The _____ refers to a cognitive bias whereby the perception of a particular trait is influenced by the perception of the former traits in a sequence of interpretations.

Edward L. Thorndike was the first to support the _____ with empirical research. In a psychology study published in 1920, Thorndike asked commanding officers to rate their soldiers; Thorndike found high cross-correlation between all positive and all negative traits.

a. Halo effect
b. Sunk costs
c. Cognitive biases
d. Distinction bias

8. A _____ occurs when people attribute their successes to internal or personal factors but attribute their failures to situational factors beyond their control. The _____ can be seen in the common human tendency to take credit for success but to deny responsibility for failure. It may also manifest itself as a tendency for people to evaluate ambiguous information in a way that is beneficial to their interests.
   a. Pygmalion effect
   b. Self-serving bias
   c. Halo effect
   d. Fundamental attribution error

9. The 'business case for _____', theorizes that in a global marketplace, a company that employs a diverse workforce (both men and women, people of many generations, people from ethnically and racially diverse backgrounds etc.) is better able to understand the demographics of the marketplace it serves and is thus better equipped to thrive in that marketplace than a company that has a more limited range of employee demographics.

An additional corollary suggests that a company that supports the _____ of its workforce can also improve employee satisfaction, productivity and retention.

   a. Kanban
   b. Trademark
   c. Virtual team
   d. Diversity

10. The trait of _____ is a central dimension of human personality. Extraverts (also spelled extroverts) tend to be gregarious, assertive, and interested in seeking out excitement. Introverts, in contrast, tend to be more reserved, less outgoing, and less sociable.
    a. A4e
    b. AAAI
    c. A Stake in the Outcome
    d. Extraversion-introversion

11. In psychology, _____ is a major approach to the study of human personality. Trait theorists are primarily interested in the measurement of traits, which can be defined as habitual patterns of behavior, thought, and emotion. According to this perspective, traits are relatively stable over time, differ among individuals (e.g. some people are outgoing whereas others are shy), and influence behavior.
    a. Psychological statistics
    b. Psychometrics
    c. Cognitive dissonance
    d. Trait theory

Chapter 11. Foundations of Behavior in Organizations

12. _____ is one of five major domains of personality discovered by psychologists. Openness involves active imagination, aesthetic sensitivity, attentiveness to inner feelings, preference for variety, and intellectual curiosity. A great deal of psychometric research has demonstrated that these qualities are statistically correlated.
    a. Extraversion
    b. Introversion
    c. Openness to experience
    d. Introverts

13. _____ , often measured as an _____ Quotient (EQ), is a term that describes the ability, capacity, skill or (in the case of the trait _____ model) a self-perceived ability, to identify, assess, and manage the emotions of one's self, of others, and of groups. Different models have been proposed for the definition of _____ and disagreement exists as to how the term should be used. Despite these disagreements, which are often highly technical, the ability _____ and trait _____ models (but not the mixed models) are enjoying considerable support in the literature and have successful applications in many different domains.
    a. A4e
    b. AAAI
    c. A Stake in the Outcome
    d. Emotional intelligence

14. _____ is one of the managerial functions like planning, organizing, staffing and directing. It is an important function because it helps to check the errors and to take the corrective action so that deviation from standards are minimized and stated goals of the organization are achieved in desired manner. According to modern concepts, _____ is a foreseeing action whereas earlier concept of _____ was used only when errors were detected. _____ in management means setting standards, measuring actual performance and taking corrective action.
    a. Decision tree pruning
    b. Turnover
    c. Schedule of reinforcement
    d. Control

15.

_____ is a commonly used, yet poorly defined concept in industrial and organizational psychology, the branch of psychology that deals with the workplace. It most commonly refers to whether a person performs their job well. Despite the confusion over how it should be exactly defined, performance is an extremely important criterion that relates to organizational outcomes and success.

a. 28-hour day
b. 33 Strategies of War
c. 1990 Clean Air Act
d. Job performance

16. _____ is a term in psychology which refers to a person's belief about what causes the good or bad results in his or her life, either in general or in a specific area such as health or academics. Understanding of the concept was developed by Julian B. Rotter in 1954, and has since become an important aspect of personality studies.

_____ refers to the extent to which individuals believe that they can control events that affect them.

a. Social loafing
b. Machiavellianism
c. Self-enhancement
d. Locus of Control

17. _____ is, according to the OED, 'the employment of cunning and duplicity in statecraft or in general conduct', deriving from the Italian Renaissance diplomat and writer Niccolò Machiavelli, who wrote Il Principe and other works. Machiavellian and variants became very popular in the late 16th century in English, though '_____' itself is first cited by the OED from 1626. The word has a similar use in modern psychology.
a. Self-enhancement
b. Machiavellianism
c. Personal space
d. Persuasion

18. _____ are, simply put, various approaches or ways of learning. They involve educating methods, particular to an individual, that are presumed to allow that individual to learn best. It is commonly believed that most people favor some particular method of interacting with, taking in, and processing stimuli or information.
a. 33 Strategies of War
b. 1990 Clean Air Act
c. 28-hour day
d. Learning styles

19. In probability theory, a probability distribution is called _____ if its cumulative distribution function is _____. This is equivalent to saying that for random variables X with the distribution in question, Pr[X = a] = 0 for all real numbers a, i.e.: the probability that X attains the value a is zero, for any number a. If the distribution of X is _____ then X is called a _____ random variable.

a. Pay Band
b. Connectionist expert systems
c. Continuous
d. Decision tree pruning

20. A _____ is the term given to a company that facilitates the learning of its members and continuously transforms itself. _____s develop as a result of the pressures facing modern organizations and enables them to remain competitive in the business environment. A _____ has five main features; systems thinking, personal mastery, mental models, shared vision and team learning.
   a. Learning Organization
   b. 1990 Clean Air Act
   c. Hoshin Kanri
   d. Quality function deployment

21. A _____ is the belief that there is a technique, method, process, activity, incentive or reward that is more effective at delivering a particular outcome than any other technique, method, process, etc. The idea is that with proper processes, checks, and testing, a desired outcome can be delivered with fewer problems and unforeseen complications. _____s can also be defined as the most efficient (least amount of effort) and effective (best results) way of accomplishing a task, based on repeatable procedures that have proven themselves over time for large numbers of people.
   a. Fix it twice
   b. Best practice
   c. Design management
   d. Hierarchical organization

22. In economics, _____ is the desire to own something and the ability to pay for it. The term _____ signifies the ability or the willingness to buy a particular commodity at a given point of time.
   a. 1990 Clean Air Act
   b. 28-hour day
   c. 33 Strategies of War
   d. Demand

23. '_____ is a conflict among the roles corresponding to two or more statuses.'

_____ is a special form of social conflict that takes place when one is forced to take on two different and incompatible roles at the same time. Consider the example of a doctor who is himself a patient, or who must decide whether he should be present for his daughter's birthday party (in his role as 'father') or attend an ailing patient (as 'doctor'.) (Also compare the psychological concept of cognitive dissonance.)

a. Social network analysis
b. Soft skill
c. Self-disclosure
d. Role conflict

24. In economics, business, retail, and accounting, a _____ is the value of money that has been used up to produce something, and hence is not available for use anymore. In economics, a _____ is an alternative that is given up as a result of a decision. In business, the _____ may be one of acquisition, in which case the amount of money expended to acquire it is counted as _____.
a. Fixed costs
b. Cost overrun
c. Cost allocation
d. Cost

Chapter 12. Leadership in Organizations

1. _____ has been described as the 'process of social influence in which one person can enlist the aid and support of others in the accomplishment of a common task' . A definition more inclusive of followers comes from Alan Keith of Genentech who said '_____ is ultimately about creating a way for people to contribute to making something extraordinary happen.'

_____ is one of the most salient aspects of the organizational context. However, defining _____ has been challenging.

   a. 1990 Clean Air Act
   b. 28-hour day
   c. Situational leadership
   d. Leadership

2. _____ is individual power based on a high level of identification with, admiration of, or respect for the powerholder.

Nationalism, Patriotism, Celebrities and well-respected people are examples of _____ in effect.

_____ is one of the Five Bases of Social Power, as defined by Bertram Raven and his colleagues[1] in 1959.

   a. 33 Strategies of War
   b. 1990 Clean Air Act
   c. 28-hour day
   d. Referent power

3. In business and accounting, _____s are everything of value that is owned by a person or company. Any property or object of value that one possesses, usually considered as applicable to the payment of one's debts is considered an _____. Simplistically stated, _____s are things of value that can be readily converted into cash.
   a. A4e
   b. AAAI
   c. A Stake in the Outcome
   d. Asset

4. _____ refers to increasing the spiritual, political, social or economic strength of individuals and communities. It often involves the empowered developing confidence in their own capacities.

The term Human _____ covers a vast landscape of meanings, interpretations, definitions and disciplines ranging from psychology and philosophy to the highly commercialized Self-Help industry and Motivational sciences.

a. A Stake in the Outcome
b. AAAI
c. A4e
d. Empowerment

5. _____ is a class of behavioural theory that claims that there is no best way to organize a corporation, to lead a company, or to make decisions. Instead, the optimal course of action is contingent (dependant) upon the internal and external situation. Several contingency approaches were developed concurrently in the late 1960s.

   a. Contingency theory
   b. Capability management
   c. Distributed management
   d. Commercial management

6. _____ in its literal sense is the process of transformation of local or regional phenomena into global ones. It can be described as a process by which the people of the world are unified into a single society and function together.

This process is a combination of economic, technological, sociocultural and political forces.

   a. Cost Management
   b. Histogram
   c. Globalization
   d. Collaborative Planning, Forecasting and Replenishment

7. The _____, is a situational leadership theory developed by Paul Hersey, a professor who wrote a well known book 'Situational Leader' and Ken Blanchard, the management guru who later became famous for his 'One Minute Manager' series. They created a model of situational leadership in the late 1960s in their work Management of Organizational Behavior (now in its 9th edition) that allows one to analyze the needs of the situation, then adopt the most appropriate leadership style. It has been proven popular with managers over the years because it is simple to understand, and it works in most environments for most people.

   a. Cross-functional team
   b. Hersey-Blanchard situational theory
   c. Human relations
   d. Goal-setting theory

8. Contingency leadership theory in organizational studies is a type of leadership theory, leadership style, and leadership model that presumes that different leadership styles are contingent to different situations. It is also referred as Situational Leadership^A® theory although, as originally convened, the _____ term is much more restrictive. The original _____ argues that the best type of leadership is totally determined by the situational variables.Currently there are many styles of leadership.
   a. Situational theory
   b. 28-hour day
   c. Situational leadership
   d. 1990 Clean Air Act

9. The _____ is a leadership theory in the field of organizational studies developed by Robert House in 1971 and revised in 1996. The theory that a leader's behavior is contingent to the satisfaction, motivation and performance of subordinates. The revised version also argues that the leader engage in behaviors that complement subordinate's abilities and compensate for deficiencies.
   a. Sociotechnical systems
   b. Human relations
   c. Corporate Culture
   d. Path-goal theory

10. The 'business case for _____', theorizes that in a global marketplace, a company that employs a diverse workforce (both men and women, people of many generations, people from ethnically and racially diverse backgrounds etc.) is better able to understand the demographics of the marketplace it serves and is thus better equipped to thrive in that marketplace than a company that has a more limited range of employee demographics.

An additional corollary suggests that a company that supports the _____ of its workforce can also improve employee satisfaction, productivity and retention.

   a. Virtual team
   b. Kanban
   c. Trademark
   d. Diversity

11.

The terms _____ and positive action refer to policies that take race, ethnicity, or gender into consideration in an attempt to promote equal opportunity. The focus of such policies ranges from employment and education to public contracting and health programs. The impetus towards _____ is twofold: to maximize diversity in all levels of society, along with its presumed benefits, and to redress perceived disadvantages due to overt, institutional, or involuntary discrimination.

a. Adam Smith
b. Affiliation
c. Abraham Harold Maslow
d. Affirmative action

12. A _____ is the belief that there is a technique, method, process, activity, incentive or reward that is more effective at delivering a particular outcome than any other technique, method, process, etc. The idea is that with proper processes, checks, and testing, a desired outcome can be delivered with fewer problems and unforeseen complications. _____s can also be defined as the most efficient (least amount of effort) and effective (best results) way of accomplishing a task, based on repeatable procedures that have proven themselves over time for large numbers of people.
   a. Fix it twice
   b. Design management
   c. Hierarchical organization
   d. Best practice

Chapter 13. Motivation in Organizations

1. A _____ is a compensation, usually financial, received by a worker in exchange for their labor.

Compensation in terms of _____s is given to worker and compensation in terms of salary is given to employees. Compensation is a monetary benefits given to employees in returns of the services provided by them.

a. Profit-sharing agreement
b. State Compensation Insurance Fund
c. Wage
d. Performance-related pay

2. _____ describes commerce transactions between businesses, such as between a manufacturer and a wholesaler, or between a wholesaler and a retailer. Contrasting terms are business-to-consumer (B2C) and business-to-government (B2G.)

The volume of B2B transactions is much higher than the volume of B2C transactions.

a. Product bundling
b. Category management
c. Market environment
d. Business-to-business

3. In business and accounting, _____s are everything of value that is owned by a person or company. Any property or object of value that one possesses, usually considered as applicable to the payment of one's debts is considered an _____. Simplistically stated, _____s are things of value that can be readily converted into cash.

a. A Stake in the Outcome
b. Asset
c. AAAI
d. A4e

4. _____, commonly known as e-commerce, consists of the buying and selling of products or services over electronic systems such as the Internet and other computer networks. The amount of trade conducted electronically has grown extraordinarily with widespread Internet usage. The use of commerce is conducted in this way, spurring and drawing on innovations in electronic funds transfer, supply chain management, Internet marketing, online transaction processing, electronic data interchange (EDI), inventory management systems, and automated data collection systems.

a. A4e
b. Electronic Commerce
c. Online shopping
d. A Stake in the Outcome

5. _____ is a theory of management that analyzes and synthesizes workflows, with the objective of improving labour productivity. The core ideas of the theory were developed by Frederick Winslow Taylor in the 1880s and 1890s, and were first published in his monographs, Shop Management and The Principles of _____ Taylor believed that decisions based upon tradition and rules of thumb should be replaced by precise procedures developed after careful study of an individual at work.

   a. Value engineering
   b. Capacity planning
   c. Master production schedule
   d. Scientific management

6. _____ Movement refers to those researchers of organizational development who study the behavior of people in groups, in particular workplace groups. It originated in the 1920s' Hawthorne studies, which examined the effects of social relations, motivation and employee satisfaction on factory productivity. The movement viewed workers in terms of their psychology and fit with companies, rather than as interchangeable parts.

   a. Hersey-Blanchard situational theory
   b. Participatory management
   c. Work design
   d. Human relations

7. In operant conditioning, _____ occurs when an event following a response causes an increase in the probability of that response occurring in the future. Response strength can be assessed by measures such as the frequency with which the response is made (for example, a pigeon may peck a key more times in the session), or the speed with which it is made (for example, a rat may run a maze faster.) The environment change contingent upon the response is called a reinforcer.

   a. Historiometry
   b. Meetings, Incentives, Conferences, and Exhibitions
   c. Diminishing Manufacturing Sources and Material Shortages
   d. Reinforcement

8. Clayton Paul Alderfer is an American psychologist who further expanded Maslow's hierarchy of needs by categorizing the hierarchy into his _____ Alderfer categorized the lower order needs (Physiological and Safety) into the Existence category. He fit Maslow's interpersonal love and esteem needs into the relatedness category. The growth category contained the Self Actualization and self esteem needs.

Alderfer also proposed a regression theory to go along with the _____. He said that when needs in a higher category are not met then individuals redouble the efforts invested in a lower category need.

a. Abraham Harold Maslow
b. ERG theory
c. Adam Smith
d. Alvin Neill Jackson

9. _____ was developed by Frederick Herzberg, a psychologist who found that job satisfaction and job dissatisfaction acted independently of each other. _____ states that there are certain factors in the workplace that cause job satisfaction, while a separate set of factors cause dissatisfaction.
   a. 1990 Clean Air Act
   b. Need for power
   c. Two-factor theory
   d. Need for Achievement

10. _____ are job factors that can cause dissatisfaction if missing but do not necessarily motivate employees if increased.

_____ have mostly to do with the job environment. These factors are important or notable only when they are lacking.

   a. Work-at-home scheme
   b. Split shift
   c. Work system
   d. Hygiene factors

11. _____ attempts to explain relational satisfaction in terms of perceptions of fair/unfair distributions of resources within interpersonal relationships. _____ is considered as one of the justice theories, It was first developed in 1962 by John Stacey Adams, a workplace and behavioral psychologist, who asserted that employees seek to maintain equity between the inputs that they bring to a job and the outcomes that they receive from it against the perceived inputs and outcomes of others (Adams, 1965.) The belief is that people value fair treatment which causes them to be motivated to keep the fairness maintained within the relationships of their co-workers and the organization.
   a. A Stake in the Outcome
   b. Equity theory
   c. AAAI
   d. A4e

Chapter 13. Motivation in Organizations

12. A _____ is the belief that there is a technique, method, process, activity, incentive or reward that is more effective at delivering a particular outcome than any other technique, method, process, etc. The idea is that with proper processes, checks, and testing, a desired outcome can be delivered with fewer problems and unforeseen complications. _____s can also be defined as the most efficient (least amount of effort) and effective (best results) way of accomplishing a task, based on repeatable procedures that have proven themselves over time for large numbers of people.

   a. Best practice
   b. Design management
   c. Hierarchical organization
   d. Fix it twice

13. _____ is about the mental processes regarding choice, or choosing. It explains the processes that an individual undergoes to make choices. In organizational behavior study, _____ is a motivation theory first proposed by Victor Vroom of the Yale School of Management.

   a. Expectancy theory
   b. AAAI
   c. A Stake in the Outcome
   d. A4e

14. The _____ is a leadership theory in the field of organizational studies developed by Robert House in 1971 and revised in 1996. The theory that a leader's behavior is contingent to the satisfaction, motivation and performance of subordinates. The revised version also argues that the leader engage in behaviors that complement subordinate's abilities and compensate for deficiencies.

   a. Sociotechnical systems
   b. Human relations
   c. Corporate Culture
   d. Path-goal theory

15. _____ is the use of empirically demonstrated behavior change techniques to improve behavior, such as altering an individual's behaviors and reactions to stimuli through positive and negative reinforcement of adaptive behavior and/or the reduction of maladaptive behavior through punishment and/or therapy.

   The first use of the term _____ appears to have been by Edward Thorndike in 1911

   a. 33 Strategies of War
   b. Behavior modification
   c. 1990 Clean Air Act
   d. 28-hour day

16. In probability theory, a probability distribution is called _____ if its cumulative distribution function is _____. This is equivalent to saying that for random variables X with the distribution in question, Pr[X = a] = 0 for all real numbers a, i.e.: the probability that X attains the value a is zero, for any number a. If the distribution of X is _____ then X is called a _____ random variable.
   a. Connectionist expert systems
   b. Pay Band
   c. Decision tree pruning
   d. Continuous

17. When an animal's surroundings are controlled, its behavior patterns after reinforcement become predictable, even for very complex behavior patterns. A schedule of reinforcement is the protocol for determining when responses or behaviors will be reinforced, ranging from _____, in which every response is reinforced, and extinction, in which no response is reinforced. Between these extremes is intermittent or partial reinforcement where only some responses are reinforced.
   a. Recognition-primed decision
   b. Pension System
   c. Continuous reinforcement
   d. Clinical decision support systems

18. When an animal's surroundings are controlled, its behavior patterns after reinforcement become predictable, even for very complex behavior patterns. A _____ is the protocol for determining when responses or behaviors will be reinforced, ranging from continuous reinforcement, in which every response is reinforced, and extinction, in which no response is reinforced. Between these extremes is intermittent or partial reinforcement where only some responses are reinforced.
   a. Control
   b. Procter ' Gamble Co.
   c. Schedule of reinforcement
   d. Linear regression

19. In organizational development (OD), _____ is the application of Socio-Technical Systems principles and techniques to the humanization of work.

The aims of _____ to improved job satisfaction, to improved through-put, to improved quality and to reduced employee problems, e.g., grievances, absenteeism.

Under scientific management people would be directed by reason and the problems of industrial unrest would be appropriately (i.e., scientifically) addressed.

a. Graduate recruitment
b. Management process
c. Path-goal theory
d. Work design

20. _____ means increasing the scope of a job through extending the range of its job duties and responsibilities. This contradicts the principles of specialisation and the division of labour whereby work is divided into small units, each of which is performed repetitively by an individual worker. Some motivational theories suggest that the boredom and alienation caused by the division of labour can actually cause efficiency to fall.

a. Job enlargement
b. Mock interview
c. Delayering
d. Centralization

21. _____ is an approach to management development where an individual is moved through a schedule of assignments designed to give him or her a breadth of exposure to the entire operation.

_____ is also practiced to allow qualified employees to gain more insights into the processes of a company, and to reduce boredom and increase job satisfaction through job variation.

The term _____ can also mean the scheduled exchange of persons in offices, especially in public offices, prior to the end of incumbency or the legislative period.

a. 1990 Clean Air Act
b. Job rotation
c. 33 Strategies of War
d. 28-hour day

22. In mathematical logic, _____ is a valid argument and rule of inference which makes the inference that, if the conjunction A and B is true, then A is true, and B is true.

In formal language:

$$A \wedge B \vdash A$$

or

$$A \wedge B \vdash B$$

The argument has one premise, namely a conjunction, and one often uses _____ in longer arguments to derive one of the conjuncts.

An example in English:

It's raining and it's pouring.

a. Validity
b. 1990 Clean Air Act
c. Fuzzy logic
d. Simplification

23. _____ is an attempt to motivate employees by giving them the opportunity to use the range of their abilities. It is an idea that was developed by the American psychologist Frederick Herzberg in the 1950s. It can be contrasted to job enlargement which simply increases the number of tasks without changing the challenge.
a. C-A-K-E
b. Cash cow
c. Catfish effect
d. Job enrichment

24. In game theory, an _____ is a set of moves or strategies taken by the players, or their payoffs resulting from the actions or strategies taken by all players. The two are complementary in that given knowledge of the set of strategies of all players, the final state of the game is known, as are any relevant payoffs. In a game where chance or a random event is involved, the _____ is not known from only the set of strategies, but is only realized when the random event(s) are realized.
a. Outcome
b. AAAI
c. A Stake in the Outcome
d. A4e

25. _____ refers to increasing the spiritual, political, social or economic strength of individuals and communities. It often involves the empowered developing confidence in their own capacities.

The term Human _____ covers a vast landscape of meanings, interpretations, definitions and disciplines ranging from psychology and philosophy to the highly commercialized Self-Help industry and Motivational sciences.

a. A4e
b. AAAI
c. A Stake in the Outcome
d. Empowerment

26. The 'business case for _____', theorizes that in a global marketplace, a company that employs a diverse workforce (both men and women, people of many generations, people from ethnically and racially diverse backgrounds etc.) is better able to understand the demographics of the marketplace it serves and is thus better equipped to thrive in that marketplace than a company that has a more limited range of employee demographics.

An additional corollary suggests that a company that supports the _____ of its workforce can also improve employee satisfaction, productivity and retention.

a. Kanban
b. Virtual team
c. Diversity
d. Trademark

Chapter 14. Communicating in Organizations

1. _____ is the systematic planning, implementing, monitoring, and revision of all the channels of communication within an organization, and between organizations; it also includes the organization and dissemination of new communication directives connected with an organization, network, or communications technology. Aspects of _____ include developing corporate communication strategies, designing internal and external communications directives, and managing the flow of information, including online communication. New technology forces constant innovation on the part of communications managers.
   a. Affiliation
   b. Adam Smith
   c. Abraham Harold Maslow
   d. Communications Management

2. An _____ is a private computer network that uses Internet technologies to securely share any part of an organization's information or operational systems with its employees. Sometimes the term refers only to the organization's internal website, but often it is a more extensive part of the organization's computer infrastructure and private websites are an important component and focal point of internal communication and collaboration.

   An _____ is built from the same concepts and technologies used for the Internet, such as client-server computing and the Internet Protocol Suite (TCP/IP.)

   a. A4e
   b. Intranet
   c. AAAI
   d. A Stake in the Outcome

3. _____ is a form of social influence. It is the process of guiding people and oneself toward the adoption of an idea, attitude, or action by rational and symbolic (though not always logical) means. It is strategy of problem-solving relying on 'appeals' rather than coercion.
   a. Personal space
   b. Self-enhancement
   c. Social loafing
   d. Persuasion

4. _____ describes the situation when output from (or information about the result of) an event or phenomenon in the past will influence the same event/phenomenon in the present or future. When an event is part of a chain of cause-and-effect that forms a circuit or loop, then the event is said to 'feed back' into itself.

Chapter 14. Communicating in Organizations

_____ is also a synonym for:

- _____ signal; the information about the initial event that is the basis for subsequent modification of the event.
- _____ loop; the causal path that leads from the initial generation of the _____ signal to the subsequent modification of the event.

_____ is a mechanism, process or signal that is looped back to control a system within itself. Such a loop is called a _____ loop.

a. Feedback
b. 1990 Clean Air Act
c. Feedback loop
d. Positive feedback

5. _____ is a subfield of the larger discipline of communication studies. _____, as a field, is the consideration, analysis, and criticism of the role of communication in organizational contexts.

The field traces its lineage through business information, business communication, and early mass communication studies published in the 1930s through the 1950s.

a. A4e
b. AAAI
c. A Stake in the Outcome
d. Organizational Communication

6. Organizational culture is not the same as _____. It is wider and deeper concepts, something that an organization 'is' rather than what it 'has' (according to Buchanan and Huczynski.)

_____ is the total sum of the values, customs, traditions and meanings that make a company unique.

a. Path-goal theory
b. Work design
c. Job analysis
d. Corporate culture

Chapter 15. Teamwork in Organizations

1. A _____ is a group of employees from various functional areas of the organization - research, engineering, marketing, finance. human resources, and operations, for example - who are all focused on a specific objective and are responsible to work as a team to improve coordination and innovation across divisions and resolve mutual problems.
    a. Graduate recruitment
    b. Goal-setting theory
    c. Cross-functional team
    d. Sociotechnical systems

2. A _____ -- also known as a geographically dispersed team -- is a group of individuals who work across time, space, and organizational boundaries with links strengthened by webs of communication technology. They have complementary skills and are committed to a common purpose, have interdependent performance goals, and share an approach to work for which they hold themselves mutually accountable. Geographically dispersed teams allow organizations to hire and retain the best people regardless of location.
    a. Kanban
    b. Virtual team
    c. Risk management
    d. Trademark

3. _____ is a civil designation for persons who are incorporated in a fixed or permanent way to a society or group: regular member of the working staff, permanent staff distinguished from a supernumerary.

   The term '_____' and its counterpart, 'supernumerary,' originated in Spanish and Latin American academy and government; it is now also used in countries all over the world, such as France, the U.S., England, Italy, etc.

   There are _____ members of surgical organizations, of universities, of gastronomical associations, etc.

    a. Abraham Harold Maslow
    b. Adam Smith
    c. Affiliation
    d. Numerary

4. _____ refers to metrics and measures of output from production processes, per unit of input. Labor _____, for example, is typically measured as a ratio of output per labor-hour, an input. _____ may be conceived of as a metrics of the technical or engineering efficiency of production.
    a. Master production schedule
    b. Value engineering
    c. Remanufacturing
    d. Productivity

Chapter 15. Teamwork in Organizations

5. In game theory, an _____ is a set of moves or strategies taken by the players, or their payoffs resulting from the actions or strategies taken by all players. The two are complementary in that given knowledge of the set of strategies of all players, the final state of the game is known, as are any relevant payoffs. In a game where chance or a random event is involved, the _____ is not known from only the set of strategies, but is only realized when the random event(s) are realized.
   a. A Stake in the Outcome
   b. AAAI
   c. Outcome
   d. A4e

6. _____ is a recursive process where two or more people or organizations work together in an intersection of common goals -- for example, an intellectual endeavor that is creative in nature--by sharing knowledge, learning and building consensus. _____ does not require leadership and can sometimes bring better results through decentralization and egalitarianism. In particular, teams that work collaboratively can obtain greater resources, recognition and reward when facing competition for finite resources._____ is also present in opposing goals exhibiting the notion of adversarial _____, though this is not a common case for using the term.
   a. Collaboration
   b. 1990 Clean Air Act
   c. 28-hour day
   d. Collectivism

7. _____ refers to the long-term management of intractable conflicts. It is the label for the variety of ways by which people handle grievances--standing up for what they consider to be right and against what they consider to be wrong. Those ways include such diverse phenomena as gossip, ridicule, lynching, terrorism, warfare, feuding, genocide, law, mediation, and avoidance.
   a. 28-hour day
   b. 1990 Clean Air Act
   c. 33 Strategies of War
   d. Conflict management

8. _____, a form of alternative dispute resolution (ADR) or 'appropriate dispute resolution', aims to assist two (or more) disputants in reaching an agreement. The parties themselves determine the conditions of any settlements reached-- rather than accepting something imposed by a third party. The disputes may involve (as parties) states, organizations, communities, individuals or other representatives with a vested interest in the outcome.
   a. Meritor Savings Bank v. Vinson
   b. Mediation
   c. Foreign Corrupt Practices Act
   d. Maximum medical improvement

9. _____ measures one's mastery of the concepts needed to perform certain work.

_____ is a complex concept that includes elements of both ability (capacity to learn) and seniority (opportunity to learn.) It is usually measured with a paper-and-pencil test.

a. Personnel management
b. Job knowledge
c. Revolving door syndrome
d. Performance appraisal

10. In the social psychology of groups, _____ is the phenomenon of people making less effort to achieve a goal when they work in a group than when they work alone. This is seen as one of the main reasons groups are sometimes less productive than the combined performance of their members working as individuals.

- Ringelmann, Max : 1913

Research began in 1913 with Max Ringelmann's study. He found that when he asked a group of men to pull on a rope, that they did not pull as hard, or put as much effort into the activity, as they did when they were pulling alone.

a. Self-enhancement
b. Personal space
c. Machiavellianism
d. Social loafing

11. In economics, business, retail, and accounting, a _____ is the value of money that has been used up to produce something, and hence is not available for use anymore. In economics, a _____ is an alternative that is given up as a result of a decision. In business, the _____ may be one of acquisition, in which case the amount of money expended to acquire it is counted as _____.
a. Cost allocation
b. Cost
c. Cost overrun
d. Fixed costs

12. A _____ is someone who helps a group of people understand their common objectives and assists them to plan to achieve them without taking a particular position in the discussion. The _____ will try to assist the group in achieving a consensus on any disagreements that preexist or emerge in the meeting so that it has a strong basis for future action. The role has been likened to that of a midwife who assists in the process of birth but is not the producer of the end result.

Chapter 15. Teamwork in Organizations

a. 1990 Clean Air Act
b. Facilitator
c. 33 Strategies of War
d. 28-hour day

13. _____ is a method by which the job performance of an employee is evaluated _____ is a part of career development.

_____s are regular reviews of employee performance within organizations

Generally, the aims of a _____ are to:

- Give feedback on performance to employees.
- Identify employee training needs.
- Document criteria used to allocate organizational rewards.
- Form a basis for personnel decisions: salary increases, promotions, disciplinary actions, etc.
- Provide the opportunity for organizational diagnosis and development.
- Facilitate communication between employee and administraton
- Validate selection techniques and human resource policies to meet federal Equal Employment Opportunity requirements.

A common approach to assessing performance is to use a numerical or scalar rating system whereby managers are asked to score an individual against a number of objectives/attributes. In some companies, employees receive assessments from their manager, peers, subordinates and customers while also performing a self assessment.

a. Personnel management
b. Human resource management
c. Progressive discipline
d. Performance appraisal

14. _____ is a broad label that refers to any individuals or households that use goods and services generated within the economy. The concept of a _____ is used in different contexts, so that the usage and significance of the term may vary.

Typically when business people and economists talk of _____s they are talking about person as _____, an aggregated commodity item with little individuality other than that expressed in the buy/not-buy decision.

a. Consumer
b. 1990 Clean Air Act
c. 28-hour day
d. 33 Strategies of War

15. _____ laws are designed to ensure fair competition and the free flow of truthful information in the marketplace. The laws are designed to prevent businesses that engage in fraud or specified unfair practices from gaining an advantage over competitors and may provide additional protection for the weak and unable to take care of themselves. _____ laws are a form of government regulation which protects the interests of consumers.
    a. Sarbanes-Oxley Act
    b. Comprehensive Environmental Response, Compensation, and Liability Act
    c. Consumer protection
    d. Certificate of Incorporation

16. _____ is a term defined by the Oxford English Dictionary as an individual's 'course or progress through life '. It is usually considered to pertain to remunerative work (and sometimes also formal education.)

The etymology of the term is somewhat ironic in that it comes from the Latin word carrera, which means race .

    a. Career planning
    b. Nursing shortage
    c. Career
    d. Spatial mismatch

17. _____ is one of the managerial functions like planning, organizing, staffing and directing. It is an important function because it helps to check the errors and to take the corrective action so that deviation from standards are minimized and stated goals of the organization are achieved in desired manner. According to modern concepts, _____ is a foreseeing action whereas earlier concept of _____ was used only when errors were detected. _____ in management means setting standards, measuring actual performance and taking corrective action.
    a. Turnover
    b. Control
    c. Schedule of reinforcement
    d. Decision tree pruning

Chapter 16. The Importance of Control

1. _____ is one of the managerial functions like planning, organizing, staffing and directing. It is an important function because it helps to check the errors and to take the corrective action so that deviation from standards are minimized and stated goals of the organization are achieved in desired manner. According to modern concepts, _____ is a foreseeing action whereas earlier concept of _____ was used only when errors were detected. _____ in management means setting standards, measuring actual performance and taking corrective action.

   a. Schedule of reinforcement
   b. Control
   c. Turnover
   d. Decision tree pruning

2. _____, commonly known as e-commerce, consists of the buying and selling of products or services over electronic systems such as the Internet and other computer networks. The amount of trade conducted electronically has grown extraordinarily with widespread Internet usage. The use of commerce is conducted in this way, spurring and drawing on innovations in electronic funds transfer, supply chain management, Internet marketing, online transaction processing, electronic data interchange (EDI), inventory management systems, and automated data collection systems.

   a. A4e
   b. Online shopping
   c. A Stake in the Outcome
   d. Electronic Commerce

3. _____ describes the situation when output from (or information about the result of) an event or phenomenon in the past will influence the same event/phenomenon in the present or future. When an event is part of a chain of cause-and-effect that forms a circuit or loop, then the event is said to 'feed back' into itself.

   _____ is also a synonym for:

   - _____ signal; the information about the initial event that is the basis for subsequent modification of the event.
   - _____ loop; the causal path that leads from the initial generation of the _____ signal to the subsequent modification of the event.

   _____ is a mechanism, process or signal that is looped back to control a system within itself. Such a loop is called a _____ loop.

   a. Feedback loop
   b. Feedback
   c. Positive feedback
   d. 1990 Clean Air Act

4. _____ is a method by which the job performance of an employee is evaluated _____ is a part of career development.

_____s are regular reviews of employee performance within organizations

Generally, the aims of a _____ are to:

- Give feedback on performance to employees.
- Identify employee training needs.
- Document criteria used to allocate organizational rewards.
- Form a basis for personnel decisions: salary increases, promotions, disciplinary actions, etc.
- Provide the opportunity for organizational diagnosis and development.
- Facilitate communication between employee and administraton
- Validate selection techniques and human resource policies to meet federal Equal Employment Opportunity requirements.

A common approach to assessing performance is to use a numerical or scalar rating system whereby managers are asked to score an individual against a number of objectives/attributes. In some companies, employees receive assessments from their manager, peers, subordinates and customers while also performing a self assessment.

a. Performance appraisal
b. Progressive discipline
c. Human resource management
d. Personnel management

5. A _____ is a change implemented to address a weakness identified in a management system. Normally _____s are implemented in response to a customer complaint, abnormal levels of internal nonconformity, nonconformities identified during an internal audit or adverse or unstable trends in product and process monitoring such as would be identified by SPC.

The process of determining a _____ requires identification of actions that can be taken to prevent or mitigate the weakness.

a. Zero defects
b. 1990 Clean Air Act
c. 28-hour day
d. Corrective action

6. _____ generally refers to a list of all planned expenses and revenues. It is a plan for saving and spending. A _____ is an important concept in microeconomics, which uses a _____ line to illustrate the trade-offs between two or more goods.

a. 33 Strategies of War
b. 1990 Clean Air Act
c. 28-hour day
d. Budget

7. _____ is the planning process used to determine whether a firm's long term investments such as new machinery, replacement machinery, new plants, new products, and research development projects are worth pursuing. It is budget for major capital, or investment, expenditures.

Many formal methods are used in _____, including the techniques such as

- Net present value
- Profitability index
- Internal rate of return
- Modified Internal Rate of Return
- Equivalent annuity

These methods use the incremental cash flows from each potential investment, or project. Techniques based on accounting earnings and accounting rules are sometimes used - though economists consider this to be improper - such as the accounting rate of return, and 'return on investment.' Simplified and hybrid methods are used as well, such as payback period and discounted payback period.

a. Gross profit margin
b. Gross profit
c. Restricted stock
d. Capital budgeting

8. _____ refers to metrics and measures of output from production processes, per unit of input. Labor _____, for example, is typically measured as a ratio of output per labor-hour, an input. _____ may be conceived of as a metrics of the technical or engineering efficiency of production.
a. Remanufacturing
b. Value engineering
c. Productivity
d. Master production schedule

9. In economics, _____ (TFP) is a variable which accounts for effects in total output not caused by inputs. For example, a year with unusually good weather will tend to have higher output, because bad weather hinders agricultural output. A variable like weather does not directly relate to unit inputs, so weather is considered a _____ variable.

a. Strict liability
b. Total-factor productivity
c. Collaborative Planning, Forecasting and Replenishment
d. Minimax

10. _____ is a business management strategy aimed at embedding awareness of quality in all organizational processes. _____ has been widely used in manufacturing, education, hospitals, call centers, government, and service industries, as well as NASA space and science programs.

As defined by the International Organization for Standardization (ISO):

> '_____ is a management approach for an organization, centered on quality, based on the participation of all its members and aiming at long-term success through customer satisfaction, and benefits to all members of the organization and to society.' ISO 8402:1994

One major aim is to reduce variation from every process so that greater consistency of effort is obtained. (Royse, D., Thyer, B., Padgett D., ' Logan T., 2006)

a. Quality management
b. 1990 Clean Air Act
c. Total quality management
d. 28-hour day

11. _____ can be considered to have three main components: quality control, quality assurance and quality improvement. _____ is focused not only on product quality, but also the means to achieve it. _____ therefore uses quality assurance and control of processes as well as products to achieve more consistent quality.

a. 1990 Clean Air Act
b. 28-hour day
c. Total quality management
d. Quality management

12. _____ is the process of comparing the cost, cycle time, productivity, or quality of a specific process or method to another that is widely considered to be an industry standard or best practice. Essentially, _____ provides a snapshot of the performance of your business and helps you understand where you are in relation to a particular standard. The result is often a business case for making changes in order to make improvements.

a. Cost leadership
b. Benchmarking
c. Complementors
d. Competitive heterogeneity

13. Organizational culture is not the same as _____. It is wider and deeper concepts, something that an organization 'is' rather than what it 'has' (according to Buchanan and Huczynski.)

_____ is the total sum of the values, customs, traditions and meanings that make a company unique.

a. Path-goal theory
b. Job analysis
c. Work design
d. Corporate culture

14. A _____ is a volunteer group composed of workers (or even students), usually under the leadership of their supervisor (but they can elect a team leader), who are trained to identify, analyse and solve work-related problems and present their solutions to management in order to improve the performance of the organization, and motivate and enrich the work of employees. When matured, true _____s become self-managing, having gained the confidence of management.
_____s are an alternative to the dehumanising concept of the Division of Labour, where workers or individuals are treated like robots.

a. Connectionist expert systems
b. Certified in Production and Inventory Management
c. Quality circle
d. Competency-based job descriptions

15. _____ is a business management strategy, initially implemented by Motorola, that today enjoys widespread application in many sectors of industry.

_____ seeks to improve the quality of process outputs by identifying and removing the causes of defects (errors) and variation in manufacturing and business processes. It uses a set of quality management methods, including statistical methods, and creates a special infrastructure of people within the organization ('Black Belts' etc.)

a. Six Sigma
b. Takt time
c. Theory of constraints
d. Production line

Chapter 16. The Importance of Control

16. In business and accounting, _____s are everything of value that is owned by a person or company. Any property or object of value that one possesses, usually considered as applicable to the payment of one's debts is considered an _____. Simplistically stated, _____s are things of value that can be readily converted into cash.
   a. A Stake in the Outcome
   b. Asset
   c. AAAI
   d. A4e

17. In probability theory, a probability distribution is called _____ if its cumulative distribution function is _____. This is equivalent to saying that for random variables X with the distribution in question, Pr[X = a] = 0 for all real numbers a, i.e.: the probability that X attains the value a is zero, for any number a. If the distribution of X is _____ then X is called a _____ random variable.
   a. Connectionist expert systems
   b. Pay Band
   c. Continuous
   d. Decision tree pruning

18. _____ is a management process whereby delivery (customer valued) processes are constantly evaluated and improved in the light of their efficiency, effectiveness and flexibility.

Some see it as a meta process for most management systems (Business Process Management, Quality Management, Project Management). Deming saw it as part of the 'system' whereby feedback from the process and customer were evaluated against organisational goals.

   a. Continuous Improvement Process
   b. First-mover advantage
   c. Critical Success Factor
   d. Sole proprietorship

19. _____ in its literal sense is the process of transformation of local or regional phenomena into global ones. It can be described as a process by which the people of the world are unified into a single society and function together.

This process is a combination of economic, technological, sociocultural and political forces.

   a. Cost Management
   b. Globalization
   c. Histogram
   d. Collaborative Planning, Forecasting and Replenishment

Chapter 16. The Importance of Control

20. _____ is a family of standards for quality management systems. _____ is maintained by ISO, the International Organization for Standardization and is administered by accreditation and certification bodies. The rules are updated, the time and changes in the requirements for quality, motivate change.

   a. A4e
   b. AAAI
   c. ISO 9000
   d. A Stake in the Outcome

21. _____ is a costing model that identifies activities in an organization and assigns the cost of each activity resource to all products and services according to the actual consumption by each: it assigns more indirect costs (overhead) into direct costs.

In this way an organization can establish the true cost of its individual products and services for the purposes of identifying and eliminating those which are unprofitable and lowering the prices of those which are overpriced.

In a business organization, the ABC methodology assigns an organization's resource costs through activities to the products and services provided to its customers.

   a. A Stake in the Outcome
   b. Indirect costs
   c. Activity-based costing
   d. A4e

22. In corporate finance, _____ or _____ is an estimate of true economic profit after making corrective adjustments to GAAP accounting, including deducting the opportunity cost of equity capital. _____ can be measured as Net Operating Profit After Taxes(or NOPAT) less the money cost of capital. _____ is similar in nature to that of calculating another financial performance measure - Residual Income , however, there are a few complexities involved with coming up with the elements for calculating _____ over RI such as the myriad adjustments that might be made to NOPAT before it is suitable for the formula below.

   a. Economic value added
   b. A Stake in the Outcome
   c. A4e
   d. AAAI

23. _____ is the price at which an asset would trade in a competitive Walrasian auction setting. _____ is often used interchangeably with open _____, fair value or fair _____, although these terms have distinct definitions in different standards, and may differ in some circumstances.

Chapter 16. The Importance of Control

International Valuation Standards defines _____ as 'the estimated amount for which a property should exchange on the date of valuation between a willing buyer and a willing seller in an arm's-length transaction after proper marketing wherein the parties had each acted knowledgeably, prudently, and without compulsion.'

_____ is a concept distinct from market price, which is 'the price at which one can transact', while _____ is 'the true underlying value' according to theoretical standards.

a. Market value
b. Restructuring
c. Payback period
d. Market value added

24. _____ is the difference between the current market value of a firm and the capital contributed by investors. If _____ is positive, the firm has added value. If it is negative, the firm has destroyed value.
   a. Net worth
   b. Market value added
   c. Deferred compensation
   d. Restructuring

25. _____ refers to the difference between the cost of materials purchased by a company plus the cost of the labor to assemble a product and the price at which the company sells the product. An example is the price of gasoline at the pump over the price of the oil in it. In national accounts used in macroeconomics, it refers to the contribution of the factors of production, i.e., land, labor, and capital goods, to raising the value of a product and corresponds to the incomes received by the owners of these factors.
   a. Minimum wage
   b. Rehn-Meidner Model
   c. Deregulation
   d. Value added

26. A _____ is the belief that there is a technique, method, process, activity, incentive or reward that is more effective at delivering a particular outcome than any other technique, method, process, etc. The idea is that with proper processes, checks, and testing, a desired outcome can be delivered with fewer problems and unforeseen complications. _____s can also be defined as the most efficient (least amount of effort) and effective (best results) way of accomplishing a task, based on repeatable procedures that have proven themselves over time for large numbers of people.

Chapter 16. The Importance of Control
115

   a. Hierarchical organization
   b. Design management
   c. Fix it twice
   d. Best practice

27. _____ is a management technique pioneered by Michael Phillips in San Francisco in the late '60's and early '70s. The concept's most visible success was by Jack Stack and his team at SRC Holdings and popularized in 1995 by John Case. The technique is to give employees all relevant financial information about the company so they can make better decisions as workers.

   a. A4e
   b. Open-book management
   c. A Stake in the Outcome
   d. AAAI

28. The _____ is a performance management tool for measuring whether the smaller-scale operational activities of a company are aligned with its larger-scale objectives in terms of vision and strategy.

By focusing not only on financial outcomes but also on the operational, marketing and developmental inputs to these, the _____ helps provide a more comprehensive view of a business, which in turn helps organizations act in their best long-term interests. This tool is also being used to address business response to climate change and greenhouse gas emissions.

   a. Balanced scorecard
   b. Middle management
   c. Management development
   d. Commercial management

29. A _____ or business method is a collection of related, structured activities or tasks that produce a specific service or product (serve a particular goal) for a particular customer or customers. It often can be visualized with a flowchart as a sequence of activities.

Chapter 16. The Importance of Control

There are three types of _____es:

1. Management processes, the processes that govern the operation of a system. Typical management processes include 'Corporate Governance' and 'Strategic Management'.
2. Operational processes, processes that constitute the core business and create the primary value stream. Typical operational processes are Purchasing, Manufacturing, Marketing, and Sales.
3. Supporting processes, which support the core processes. Examples include Accounting, Recruitment, Technical support.

A _____ begins with a customer's need and ends with a customer's need fulfillment. Process oriented organizations break down the barriers of structural departments and try to avoid functional silos.

 a. 1990 Clean Air Act
 b. 28-hour day
 c. 33 Strategies of War
 d. Business process

30. _____ is the provision of service to customers before, during and after a purchase.

According to Turban et al. (2002), '_____ is a series of activities designed to enhance the level of customer satisfaction - that is, the feeling that a product or service has met the customer expectation.'

Its importance varies by product, industry and customer; defective or broken merchandise can be exchanged, often only with a receipt and within a specified time frame.

 a. 28-hour day
 b. 1990 Clean Air Act
 c. Customer service
 d. Service rate

31. _____ is an advertisement in which a particular product specifically mentions a competitor by name for the express purpose of showing why the competitor is inferior to the product naming it.

This should not be confused with parody advertisements, where a fictional product is being advertised for the purpose of poking fun at the particular advertisement, nor should it be confused with the use of a coined brand name for the purpose of comparing the product without actually naming an actual competitor. ('Wikipedia tastes better and is less filling than the Encyclopedia Galactica.')

In the 1980s, during what has been referred to as the cola wars, soft-drink manufacturer Pepsi ran a series of advertisements where people, caught on hidden camera, in a blind taste test, chose Pepsi over rival Coca-Cola.

a. 28-hour day
b. 1990 Clean Air Act
c. 33 Strategies of War
d. Comparative advertising

32. _____-model (SCOR(r)) is a process reference model developed by the management consulting firm PRTM and AMR Research and endorsed by the Supply-Chain Council (SCC) as the cross-industry de facto standard diagnostic tool for supply chain management. SCOR enables users to address, improve, and communicate supply chain management practices within and between all interested parties in the Extended Enterprise.

SCOR(r) is a management tool, spanning from the supplier's supplier to the customer's customer. The model has been developed by the members of the Council on a volunteer basis to describe the business activities associated with all phases of satisfying a customer's demand.

a. Supply chain management software
b. Delayed differentiation
c. Supply Chain Risk Management
d. Supply-Chain Operations Reference

ANSWER KEY

Chapter 1
1. a   2. d   3. d   4. b   5. c   6. d   7. d   8. d   9. a   10. d
11. c   12. b   13. d   14. d   15. d   16. d   17. b   18. c   19. d   20. d
21. d   22. d   23. c   24. b   25. d   26. b   27. b   28. d   29. d   30. c
31. b   32. b   33. b   34. d   35. b   36. d   37. c   38. d   39. a   40. d
41. d   42. d   43. d   44. d   45. d   46. b   47. c

Chapter 2
1. b   2. c   3. d   4. d   5. d   6. c   7. d   8. d   9. d   10. d
11. b   12. d   13. d   14. d   15. d   16. d   17. b   18. d   19. c   20. c
21. d   22. b   23. c   24. d

Chapter 3
1. d   2. c   3. a   4. d   5. d   6. d   7. d   8. d   9. d   10. d
11. a   12. b   13. d   14. d   15. b   16. c   17. c   18. c   19. a   20. d
21. d   22. d   23. d   24. d   25. c   26. d

Chapter 4
1. d   2. c   3. d   4. c   5. d   6. c   7. b   8. c   9. c   10. b
11. d   12. d   13. a   14. d   15. c   16. d

Chapter 5
1. c   2. b   3. d   4. d   5. c   6. d   7. a   8. d   9. d   10. b
11. d   12. b

Chapter 6
1. b   2. d   3. d   4. c   5. d   6. a   7. d   8. d   9. d   10. d
11. d   12. b   13. c   14. d   15. d   16. c   17. a   18. b   19. b   20. c
21. d   22. d

Chapter 7
1. a   2. d   3. c   4. d   5. d   6. d   7. d   8. b   9. b   10. b
11. d   12. c   13. d   14. d   15. a   16. b   17. d   18. b   19. d   20. a
21. d   22. d   23. d   24. d   25. d   26. d   27. d   28. d

Chapter 8
1. d   2. a   3. d   4. b   5. b   6. d   7. d   8. d   9. c   10. a
11. d   12. a   13. b   14. c   15. d

Chapter 9
1. b   2. d   3. b   4. c   5. d   6. d   7. d   8. b   9. d   10. d
11. d   12. d   13. a   14. d   15. a   16. c   17. d   18. b   19. b   20. d
21. c   22. d   23. d   24. d   25. d   26. d   27. b   28. a   29. b   30. c
31. c   32. c   33. d   34. a   35. d   36. a   37. a   38. d   39. d   40. a
41. d   42. c   43. d   44. c   45. c   46. d   47. d

ANSWER KEY

Chapter 10
1. a   2. d   3. d   4. d   5. d   6. b   7. d   8. d   9. d   10. d
11. d   12. d   13. d   14. d   15. d   16. b   17. c   18. d   19. d   20. d
21. d   22. b   23. c   24. d   25. d

Chapter 11
1. a   2. b   3. b   4. c   5. a   6. b   7. a   8. b   9. d   10. d
11. d   12. c   13. d   14. d   15. d   16. d   17. b   18. d   19. c   20. a
21. b   22. d   23. d   24. d

Chapter 12
1. d   2. d   3. d   4. d   5. a   6. c   7. b   8. a   9. d   10. d
11. d   12. d

Chapter 13
1. c   2. d   3. b   4. b   5. d   6. d   7. d   8. b   9. c   10. d
11. b   12. a   13. a   14. d   15. b   16. d   17. c   18. c   19. d   20. a
21. b   22. d   23. d   24. a   25. d   26. c

Chapter 14
1. d   2. b   3. d   4. a   5. d   6. d

Chapter 15
1. c   2. b   3. d   4. d   5. c   6. a   7. d   8. b   9. b   10. d
11. b   12. b   13. d   14. a   15. c   16. c   17. b

Chapter 16
1. b   2. d   3. b   4. a   5. d   6. d   7. d   8. c   9. b   10. c
11. d   12. b   13. d   14. c   15. a   16. b   17. c   18. a   19. b   20. c
21. c   22. a   23. a   24. b   25. d   26. d   27. b   28. a   29. d   30. c
31. d   32. d

www.ingramcontent.com/pod-product-compliance
Lightning Source LLC
Chambersburg PA
CBHW082049230426
43670CB00016B/2828